STANZA STONES

SIMON ARMITAGE

WITH PIP HALL AND TOM LONSDALE

STANZA STONES

ENITHARMON PRESS

First published in 2013
by Enitharmon Press
10 Bury Place
London WC1A 2JL

ISBN 978-1-907587-30-6 (hardback)
ISBN 978-1-907587-49-8 (signed limited edition)

Enitharmon Press gratefully acknowledges the financial support
of Arts Council England through Grants for the Arts
and
Neptune Investment Management
who contributed toward the cost of this book.

Printed and made in Great Britain

CONTENTS

preface – simon armitage

A FULL YEAR has passed since the last Stanza Stone was craned into
position, and the seasons have done their work. Visiting them
recently, I felt as if they were now admitted and accepted forms
within the landscape, not natural features of course but as much
a part of the Pennine furniture as a wall, marker post or stile.
Heather has re-established itself around the two Puddle Stones
on Ilkley Moor where a digger had gouged open a resting place
for them in the sodden peat; moss and lichen have colonised
the letters of the Mist Stone on Nab Hill; in Backstone Beck
fluctuating water levels have brought an unexpected palette of
green algae and red oxides to the left-hand margins of the Beck
poem; the two Dew Stones on Rivock Edge have lost the sheen
of newness that initially distinguished the sawn rocks from the
ancient dry-stone walls which frame them; the full blast of the

weather has calmed and healed the long lines of the Rain poem which, when they were first carved, seemed raw and exposed; and the last time I hiked up the long straight incline of the old truck-track to the top of Pule Hill and turned into the disused quarry, the words of the Snow Stone were inlaid from first capital letter to final full-stop with ice, adamantine and almost electrically bright in the winter sun. Seeing it there, reading it, considering how it had become the embodiment of its creative intentions brought an intense feeling of achievement, and for a few self-congratulatory minutes I allowed myself to think of it as the stunningly appropriate and effortless conclusion to a long and very complicated project. I've said on many occasions that if a poem, once written, is exactly the same as its author first imagined it would be, then it is almost certainly a failure, and that artistic success must always involve a process of transformation. On that basis alone, the Stanza Stones are a success story for the simple reason that they actually exist, because until that final sun-struck, ice-shining moment I didn't really believe they were possible.

In a cold church hall at the back of Ilkley Literature Festival's terraced office in late 2010, Rachel Feldberg proposed some kind of collaboration or commission, though at that first meeting I don't recall either of us having any firm ideas. Rachel wanted the project to be immediate and participatory yet have a long-term legacy, and I'd just walked the Pennine Way, struck by the number of markings and carved signs along the route. It was probably the coming together of those ambitions and experiences that led to the notion of poems in the landscape. Or poem singular to begin with, because my original impulse was to identify an abandoned quarry face or hillside and carve huge letters into it, creating a poetic Mount Rushmore somewhere within Yorkshire. I'd worked with Antony Gormley on a couple of projects in the past and was always impressed with the scale of his ambition and the courage of his convictions when it came to situating art out of doors. Like the Great Wall of China, maybe this poem would be one of the few

man-made objects on earth to be visible from the moon…. In the end funding considerations, reality checks and a few bouts of humility forced us to redefine the parameters of Stanza Stones and rethink its aspirations, and all for the better. A new territory came into focus, that of the South Pennine Watershed, the moorland region which by a fluke of convenience happens to extend from my home village of Marsden in the south to Ilkley in the north, and a new endeavour came to mind, that of creating a suite or succession of poems to be sited at intervals across those moors, to be carved into existing or introduced stones. Everything then seemed to fall into place very quickly, from the appointment of a landscape architect and a lettercarver to the procurement of goods, services, permissions and promises, until suddenly the only thing holding back the commencement of a major public art enterprise/construction project was the small matter of half a dozen poems. When would they be ready, and what would they say?

Animated against the skyline, the Cow and Calf are two weather-sculpted rocks which form part of a longer escarpment of exposed gritstone to the north-facing ridge of Ilkley Moor. In silhouette against the horizon they have taken on an iconic significance for the town of Ilkley itself, and the nearby restaurant, café and car park testify to their popularity among picnickers, climbers, walkers, day-trippers and the like. Although the two stones themselves haven't gone unscathed, graffiti artists armed with knives or chisels have tended to favour neighbouring out-crops; many are scored with names and dates going back as far as the eighteenth century but also bear more recent contributions from courting couples, football fans and admirers of particular rock bands. Thinking of the quarry behind the Cow and Calf as a kind of gateway or portal onto the wider moor, the graffiti can be viewed as a sampler or foretaste of what lies beyond, because for many thousands of years people have been visiting this upland

region to offer their prayers and express their desires in the form of carved stones and man-made formations. Ilkley Moor and the encompassing Rombald's Moor have more such monuments than almost anywhere in the western world, from prehistoric cup-and-ring markings, to cryptically decorated and engraved rocks, to enigmatically arranged groups of standing stones. It may seem ironic but it is also of huge significance that sacred or artistic gestures like these should appear in such a high, remote and inaccessible location, appealing for the most part to an audience of nobody, presenting their ideas directly to the gods and the stars above. In many ways, both the inspiration and the permission for the Stanza Stones poems comes directly from that tradition, and the poems represent a contribution to an unbroken and ongoing dialogue which has been taking place on the open canvas or blank page of the moors from Neolithic times. Right from the outset I felt the urge to say something both particular and universal, both timely and timeless, and in a style that took its potential readership into account. Because it's one thing to publish poetry in books or journals, to preach to the converted perhaps, but something slightly different to write for a public space or to put poems in front of people who might have no experience of contemporary verse and little interest in it. And different again to compose a poem which might last for a thousand years, whose readers are…people from the future. Impossible of course to imagine such an audience or their relationship with poetry of the early 21st century, bearing in mind the way language has evolved and morphed over the preceding millennium. But a thought to conjure with all the same.

Even though I didn't have a subject in mind, my first inclination was to write a sestina, distributing the six stanzas among six different stones. The maths added up – hopefully the language would follow. Those familiar with the sestina form will know that the six end-words of each verse are repeated in a rearranged, pre-arranged pattern, so choosing the right ones is important. But as so often with a poem, the plan had to change. Every time I went to the moor I collected a bit more language until I had several long lists of terms and phrases associated with the territory. I'd choose six and begin writing, but got nowhere. On a couple of occasions I had a vague sense that a poem was beginning to take shape, but it was rarely more than three or four lines, and never that feeling of being onto something. The daydream just wouldn't go on dreaming. The crystal wouldn't coalesce. My poetic teacher, Peter Sansom, once told me that it's sometimes best to forget about a poem for a few weeks rather than struggle or fight with it, to let the subconscious put in its shift, so that's what I did, and when I returned to it with a clearer mind and a clean eye, I saw what the problems were. Firstly I was attempting something formulaic and literary rather than trusting to impulses and intuition. Secondly, the sestina framework seemed too inflexible and stubborn to accommodate the epic geographies and rich vocabulary of the moor. Thirdly, I still had no idea what the poem was trying to articulate. And lastly, I was letting the form dictate the content – a case of letting the tail wag the dog, or to use a Yorkshire phrase, putting the cart before the horse. After another visit to the hills, this time in lashing rain, I came back with a different idea and a single purpose. To let water be the overall subject: the water that sculpted the valleys, the water that powered the industries, the water we take for granted. Water – our most vital necessity, our common gold, our shaping force, and our local vintage. And to let the various forms of water provide the topic of each individual and self-contained poem. A piece about rain, a piece about snow, a piece about dew…the Rain Stone, the Snow Stone, the Dew Stone…and so on. Then a bigger, over-arching title came into my head, *In Memory of Water*. I suppose I saw an opportunity to draw on the often commemorative nature of monumental-masonry and engraving by making an unspoken connection with environmental themes and concerns about climate change. Perhaps I was thinking ahead, pessimistically, to a future where the Stanza Stones still existed but on a planet that had either drowned or boiled dry. It's impossible to say that an idea is 'right'. All I know is that no sooner had the notion occurred to me than the poems started to happen, even to the point where I was anxious to get to my notebook, because words and lines and sentences were queuing up in my head, impatient to be written down. To me this is always the most engaging phase, where the internal, abstract concept of the poem is attempting to materialise externally, where the mind is in negotiation with the world through the medium of language. What we call writing.

It's been exciting to see how others have responded to the same themes in their own writing. Over the course of several months I led groups of young poets up onto those same moors – above Marsden, above Oxenhope, above Ilkley – and gave them no particular instruction other than to collect words. And from those words, firstly through writing exercises in workshops, then later in their own time and space, poems came into being. Some of the group members were already familiar with the Pennine landscape, but others had no experience of it whatsoever, and it was impossible not to grin now and again at the sight of cool city kids in expensive trainers picking their way through peaty bogs, or to see carefully moulded hairdos being blown every-which-way by the raging wind. But eye-opening, moving and inspiring to read poems of raw experience, personal insight and genuine feeling, and to see what impression the wild landscape had made on such vivid and hungry imaginations.

The Snow Stone, the first to be carved, now forms the beginning of the 47-mile Stanza Stone Trail, a walk that utilises existing footpaths, bridleways, towpaths and other public thoroughfares to connect the poems. Or to 'collect' them, even; I haven't walked the whole trail myself, but those who have seem to task themselves with finding each poem and capturing it in the form of a photograph, and judging by internet sites and blogs the

Stanza Stones Trail has already become something of a recognised and established activity. The stones have also acquired their own guardians, walkers mainly, regular visitors who clear a few weeds away once in a while, remove litter from the sites and generally keep an eye on things. Given how exposed and vulnerable I feel the poems to be, I find their informal stewardship greatly reassuring. And also a matter of great pride, in as much as people seem to have taken possession of them, even allowed themselves to be possessed by them. Some have written about their favourite stone, and asked me to name mine, and even though it's somehow iniquitous to choose between them I have to admit that having a poem carved not just in the village where I was born but into the side of Pule Hill, a hill which loomed large over the village of Marsden and exerted such a powerful gravity over me as a child is an extraordinary privilege. I'd go there often, nearly always alone, and I remember finding snow piled up in a corner of the old quarry long after Easter and long after all other traces of winter weather had disappeared. The Snow poem, carved horizontally across two massive slabs that once formed part of a very crude wall or embankment, now strikes me as a sort of poetic Plimsoll line, daring the snow to reach the heights it once did.

The stones could be thought of as sites in their own right, literal landmarks, places to visit. Or they could be thought of as milestones or marker posts along the invisible route of the watershed. A drop of rain falling one inch to the west of the watershed will find its way to the Irish Sea, and one inch to the east to the North Sea; theoretically a person should be able to walk from Marsden to Ilkley along that crest without getting their feet wet, though I doubt this has ever been achieved. And those looking hard enough might stumble across a seventh Stanza Stone, a secret stone left in an unnamed location within the South Pennine water catchment, waiting to be discovered and read.

I want to acknowledge that Stanza Stones was not in any way the work of a single mind, but endlessly collaborative in nature,

involving, at the final count, hundreds of helpers, workers and
volunteers and thousands of hours of time, much of it given freely
and very much appreciated. So despite the name and title of the
project, I find myself remembering it not just in terms of stones
and stanzas but as a series of human encounters that took place
over a two-year period, many of them in astonishing locations
and bizarre circumstances. And as a series of conversations
ranging from the forensically detailed to the absurdly fantastical,
particularly with Rachel Feldberg, director of the Ilkley Literature
Festival, who oversaw the enterprise with extraordinary patience
and energy from beginning to end, and with landscape architect
Tom Lonsdale and with letter carver Pip Hall. After this preface
I bow out to let the poems do my bidding and to let Tom and Pip
have their own say, but I wanted to thank them first. I've met very
few people who know and respect the Pennine landscape as much

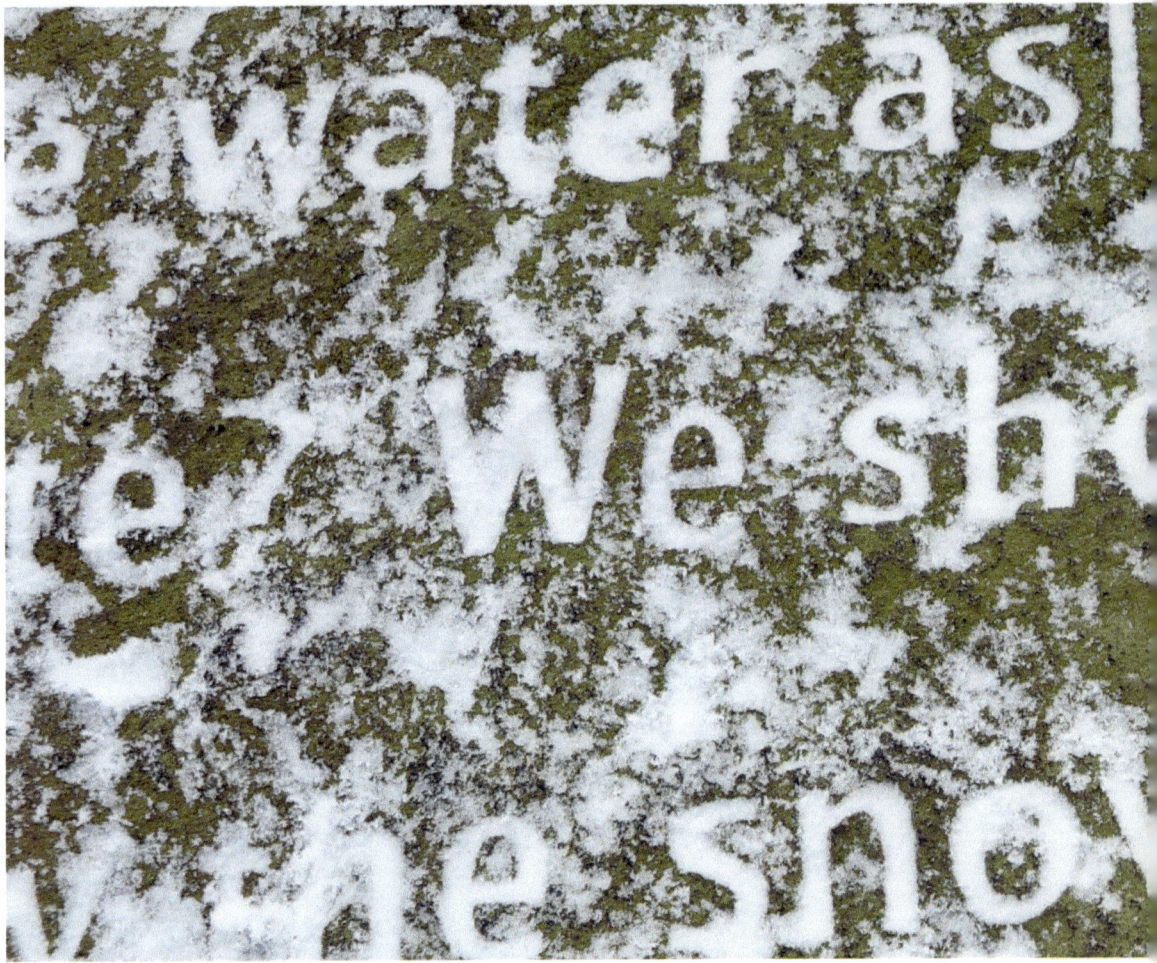

as Tom Lonsdale, or have his understanding of its geographies and its processes. Without his sympathetic judgements, professional expertise and common sense not one stone would have found its way into position, and the whole adventure was underpinned by his guidance, his good nature and his optimism. As for Pip Hall of Dentdale, she is a force of nature, and one that did battle with many other forces of nature to see the job finished. Sometimes with her apprentice Wayne Hart but often alone, working by hand and eye, in temperatures that made my fingers feel like they were going to fall off, in blinding rain, in enfolding mists, in pummelling winds, or up to her thighs in the raging torrent of Backstone Beck, she practised a combination of industry and artistry that not only defied the conditions but seemed to draw strength from them. She carved through the wettest year on

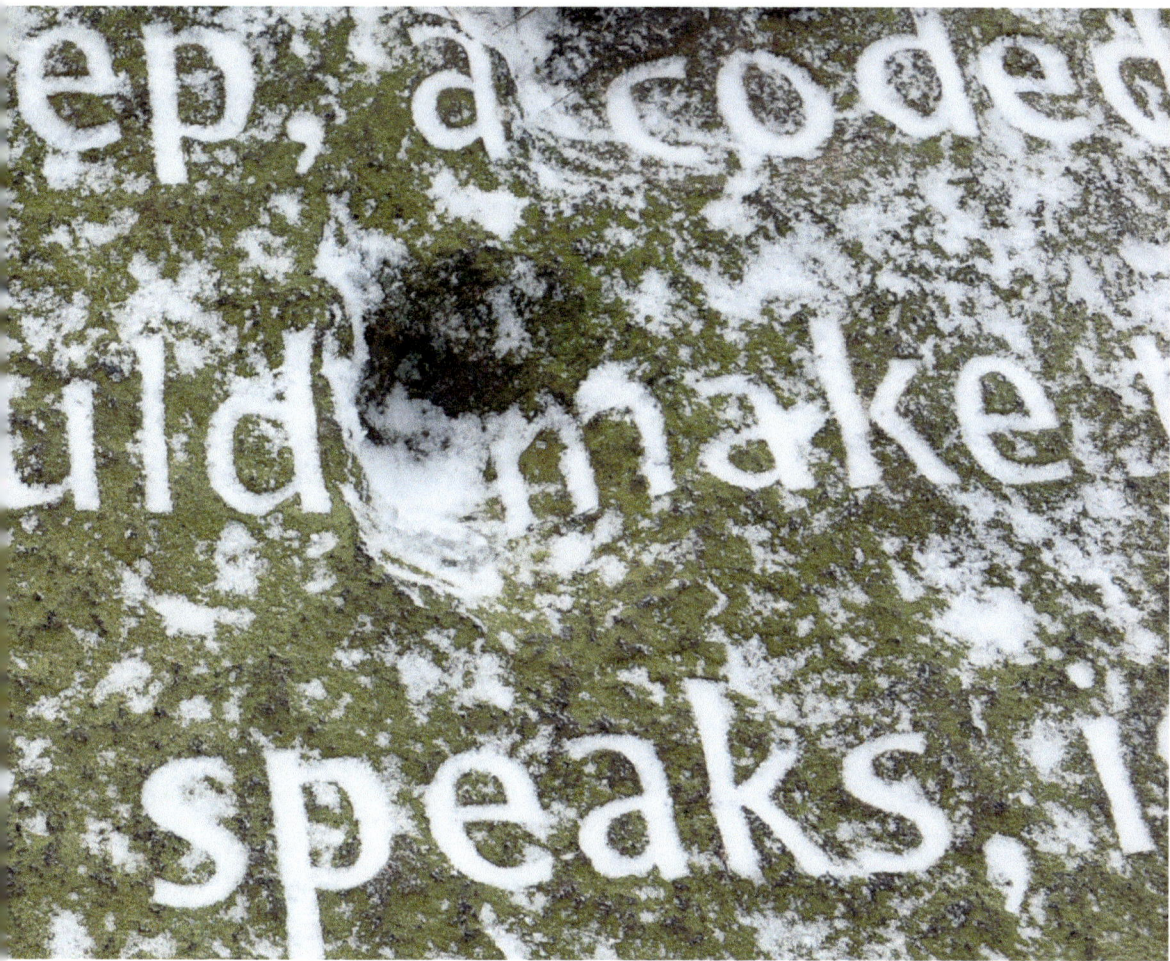

ep, a coded
uld make
speaks, i

record, which at one point caused me to wonder if the stones were somehow prophetic or visionary, and made me wish I'd written about sunshine instead, or money. But the heavens brightened every once in a while, and one morning as I walked up onto the moor, the tapping of metal on stone and the sight of her red and white scarf protecting her face and mouth from chippings and dust were the only noise and colour for several miles in any direction. When I reached the rock, the freshly-cut letters shone bold and vivid in the early light, full of oranges and yellows and sparkling with minerals. So for a few moments it seemed as if she had opened a chorus of tiny mouths in the stone, each with its own vowel or consonant, and allowed it to speak or sing.

Simon Armitage, West Yorkshire, 2013

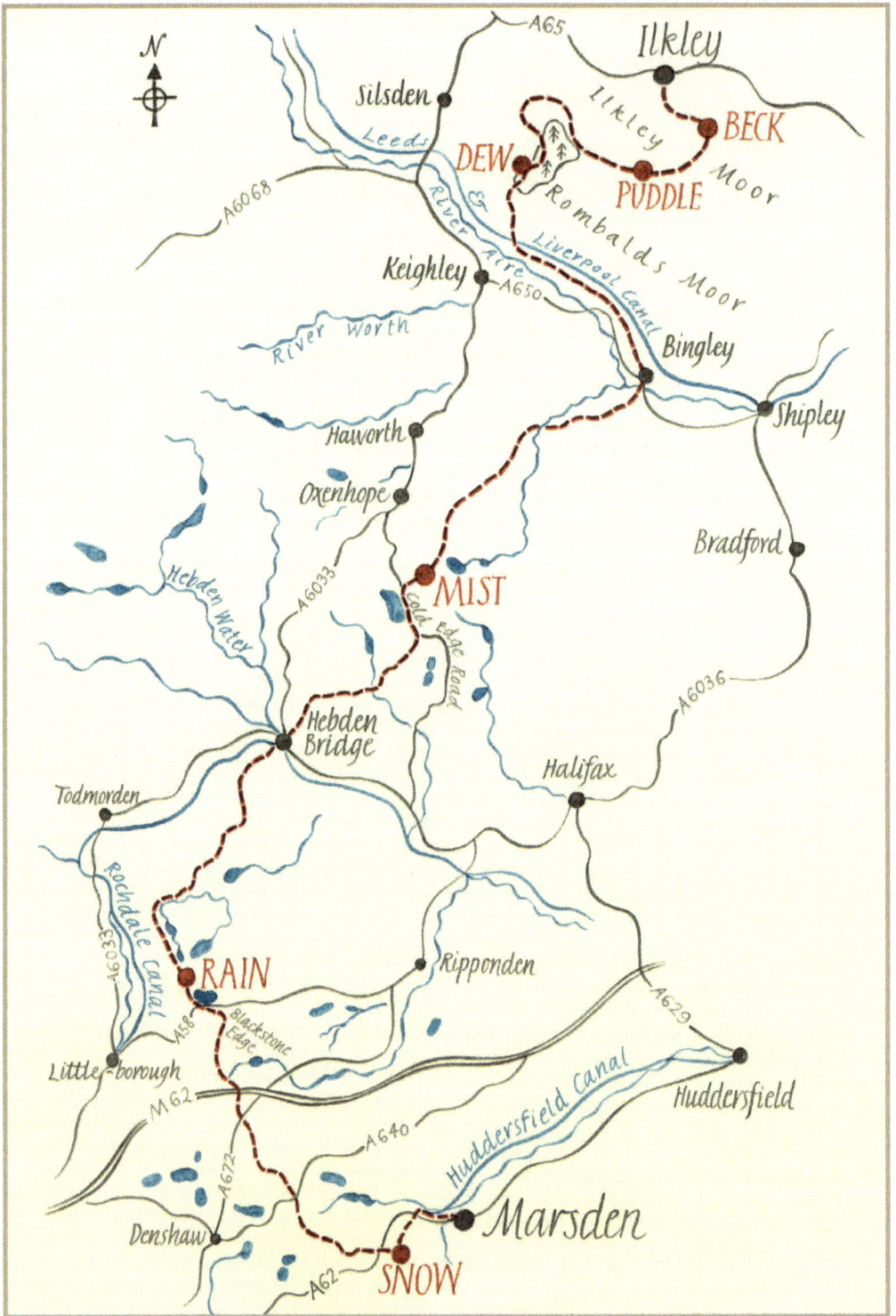

The Stanza Stones Trail

touching the landscape: tom lonsdale

where angels fear to tread

WHEN ILKLEY Literature Festival approached me with an invitation to work with Simon Armitage my first obligation was to decide whether the project was going to inflict harm or benefit on the landscape, because professionals in my line of work all take a sort of unspoken Hippocratic oath early in our careers pledging to act only in the best interests of the world around us. There was always the risk that I might turn around and insist that this was a bad thing to do, but it didn't take long to conclude that here was the chance to return something precious to a landscape that has given us so much in the past: this would be a beneficial act in a countryside that has slumbered briefly since an episode of human activity devoted to extracting its resources. We would not be inhibited by the curious trait of human nature that views any sudden change with suspicion whilst slow, creeping change is assimilated subliminally to become the state being defended. In other fields of my work as a landscape architect this crops up all the time, like the asylum afforded to self-seeded sycamore trees in a park becoming so shaded that flowers bloom no more and lone visitors feel unsafe.

The reality of bygone change in the South Pennines is that the hills have long echoed with the clamour of quarrying, water engineering construction, motorway building and farming, to say nothing of the ancient forest clearance that stripped our uplands

bare in the first place. Even the impression that these activities
have died out is unreliable as helicopters are frequently seen
carrying bales of heather to restore impoverished ground, followed
by stone flags to protect the same heather from countless walking
boots.

It was also self-evident that the physical scale and impact of Pip
Hall's carving would be almost imperceptible in comparison with
these other interventions and in relation to the vastness of the
Pennine moors, where the eyes are drawn to horizon and sky, with
objects as massive as Stoodley Pike monument figuring only as
specks in the distance until within touching range. We were talking
only of scratching away the surface of something inert that is being
constantly eroded by the forces of nature in any case: nothing
living was to suffer.

This analysis, sometimes reflected upon privately but often
discussed openly within the team, led to a very confident ethical
stance for the project. We were acting in a noble tradition of
making marks on the land, following the example set by the

unknown but revered masons who carved the Cup and Ring patterns that abound on Rombalds Moor: in a slice of wonderful irony these stones are protected by law as scheduled ancient monuments and cited as the reason that no new marks should be permitted, whilst 'Mandi' and others have their names carved into the rocks or tree bark with abandon but no permission and little artistry.

We set ourselves some guiding principles, by which we could justify to future generations that the 21st century has a worthy entry to make in the 'Book of the Land'. These principles were simple: every aspect was to embody the highest quality of content and execution, conducted with humility and sincerity. We scoured the nation's best letter-cutting artists to find some-one with the skill and sensitivity to carve the words and had no doubt that Pip was the right person. Finally the locations had to be chosen with exceptional care: each stone needed to respect its site, and each site needed to celebrate and protect the nature of the stones that would bear the poems into the distant future.

not here but there

Offering up prospective sites for Simon Armitage's approval
initially held for me much of the trepidation associated with
the *Dragons' Den* television programme. When the time came
though it turned out to be much more like a day out with a
regular walking companion, enriched by conversations in which
crucial parts of the project philosophy got talked about and
crystallised. I also confess that some beer was drunk and chat
occasionally strayed into more abstract dimensions.

Simon's request had been for sites on or near the Pennine
watershed but that is a mighty big catchment. There had to be
some limitation to the area of search, or I would still be looking,
and Rachel Feldberg made things a little easier by suggesting the

stones be sited between Simon's birthplace in Marsden and the home of the Literature Festival in Ilkley. At that stage there was no suggestion of a Stanza Stones Trail but it seemed natural to space the stones out along an imaginary line that hugged high ground between the two end-points.

We obviously needed some additional criteria in order to narrow down further what could have been aimless wanderings with a risk of hypothermia. Practical considerations naturally occupied our minds, with the prospect of carting a ton of stone across miles of bog ruling out large areas, but aesthetic judgement seemed to loom even larger: a poem discovered in a random and featureless location could seem absurd and say little to the reader. Our quest was therefore to find special spaces, possessing a distinctive sense of place that would be memorable in its own right with nothing added: in such locations sensitively introduced poetry can heighten the enjoyment of the place at the same time as drawing additional power from its setting.

The penny dropped early in this exercise that we did not need to import rock into a landscape made of the stuff and strewn with fragments of it in all shapes and sizes. By the same token there would be situations where the existing rock wouldn't offer enough of a 'page' or might prove resistant to Pip's chiselling, so we permitted ourselves the option of introducing stones to some sites and saw merit in the variety of experience this would offer readers intending to visit all of the stones.

For someone with my range of outdoor interests this whole enterprise began to feel like being paid to enjoy myself: I have a love of maps and hill walking, so time spent in preparation for and during reconnoitres was hardly an imposition. Getting to a promising site also became an excuse to ride my motorbike along the scenic lanes and byways of the South Pennines before dismounting and donning the walking boots. Thus a long list of possible sites emerged, ripe for Caesar's thumb and a second visit with Simon minus motorbike this time (he's not ready for that). Within moments of arriving at each location I could sense the decision and soon afterwards would come the words 'I'm not feeling the love, Tom' or 'It's asking for it!'

At this point we were joined in the team by Pip, whose input was essential in both final selection of sites and, more especially, which individual stone would respond to her chisels and reward the writing. Further jolly hours were spent pulling back vegetation to reveal the gritstone surfaces and assessing how she would arrange her camp and position herself to carry out this delicate task in whatever Pennine weather was in store.

you can do anything but you can't do that

It is extremely unlikely that Pip would have been arrested if she had simply gone out and carved these poems unannounced: the incidence of names and other symbols scratched, painted and chalked onto slabs and crags in the hills by anonymous scribes bears witness to that. Nevertheless, the fact remains that doing so would have ranked as a criminal act, which neither we nor our clients and patrons could contemplate, funded as we were by the public purse, plus here was an opportunity to set a fine example of how art and culture can earn its rightful place in the countryside. Hence my next task was to ensure that all appropriate permissions and endorsements were obtained and the work done in a responsible manner.

Consultation is a tricky business because it is neither possible nor desirable to have dialogue with every person in the universe who has an opinion on the subject, though thankfully there are statutory organisations such as Natural England, English Heritage and the National Trust who represent the opinions of many with one clear voice, and because our values and their values tend to coincide we were keen to seek their approval.

But the obvious first port of call is the landowner and it is not

always easy to find out who that is. In the case of the Snow Stone
it was immediately evident that the National Trust owned Pule
Hill because they erect signs where public footpaths enter their
Marsden Moor estate and Ordnance Survey also kindly mark it
with an oak sprig on their maps. The Trust's enthusiastic support
for Stanza Stones was a tremendous fillip and extended to use
of their machinery and volunteer drivers to move stone for us.
As we gradually traced and approached other landowners they
seemed to take the view that, if National Trust thought this to
be a good thing, then a good thing it must be. Utility companies
such as Yorkshire Water own large tracts of moorland catchment,
including the site for Mist Stone. In the case of the Rain Stone,
United Utilites only manage their catchment and infrastructure
on land belonging to the Lord of the Manor of Rochdale, who

turns out to live abroad, which left to us a slightly surreal exchange of correspondence through his land agent. Ilkley Moor was the most straightforward in terms of possession because, as well as owning the land, Bradford Council are partners in the project governance.

Another absentee owns the forest where the Dew Stones now reside and was sufficiently supportive to authorise his forest management contractor to give us direct assistance. This turned out to be complicated by cattle-droving easements established by custom and practice rather than written into legal documents. Complex negotiations with neighbouring farmers resulted in taking down and rebuilding drystone walls and two attempts at fixing the two very heavy stones. In the end it was the farmers themselves, especially the Boothman family, who did much of the work and the two stones now stand there with little hint of the dialogue (some of it quite florid) invested in their arrival.

Natural England provided interesting challenges and entertainment, ensuring that we did nothing that would impair the Site of Special Scientific Interest (sss1) for which they are the statutory watchdog and in which we had been careless enough to select five of the six stone sites. They were only doing their job of course and, quite correctly, they needed reassurances that we would not disrupt the ground-nesting birds whose habitat is the basis of the sss1 designation. Pip and a handful of chisels seem unlikely to reduce the bird population of the Pennines but heavy machinery was necessary for moving the imported stones for Dew and Puddle. We also wanted to lift and reposition Mist, albeit by hand, so method statements had to be written and agreed for every site and dispensations granted under the Higher Level Stewardship schemes operating. The most frustrating constraint was suspension of all work on moorland throughout the bird-nesting season, the later part of which coincides with the firm ground conditions needed for the heavy machinery and with

the best weather for Pip to be out on the moor carving *in situ.*
This influenced the programme for the whole project, with late
summer and autumn seeing most of the carving on site and
the imported stones carved under cover in winter ready for
positioning before the nesting season started.

joining up the dots

Only two of the Stanza Stones present themselves to passing
walkers in a prominent way: Rain adorns a slab on the front
edge of Cow's Mouth Quarry where the Pennine Way crosses
the delightfully named Light Hazzles Edge, and Dew greets
walkers or riders on the bridleway as it emerges from the dark
interior of Rivock Edge Forest near Silsden. The remaining
stones were not intentionally hidden from view but it was always

Simon's preference that there be an element of intrigue in finding the stones. That intrigue can be heightened rather than undermined if there is a source of information to help those interested in looking for them, so a guide of some sort was envisaged.

An element of physical exertion on the part of those seeking the stones is also consistent with the project's origins as part of the 2012 Cultural Olympiad and iMove funding. Whilst there are six individual poems, each carefully placed for its own reasons, they all belong to the same cohesive set and there is logic in the notion of a walking trail connecting them with each other and linking Marsden with Ilkley. Devising such a trail and its accompanying navigation guide became a task of similar magnitude to locating the stone sites in the first place, bearing in mind the large distances involved and the fact that the route must adhere to public rights of way or access land and, as far as possible, avoid experiences that sully the pleasure of visiting the stones. Turning this latter object on its head, there was an opportunity to use the guide to reveal many other delights to be had by walking in the South Pennines.

Map-work again preceded reconnoitres, charting public access and plausible terrain that could then be checked out physically. Adhering to high ground wherever possible works with the spirit and subject matter of the poems and affords an endless sequence of panoramic views for the walker, as well as limiting the amount of ascent and descent. In some places it is necessary to drop down and cross a valley in order to connect two stones – for instance the gorgeous Luddenden Dene lies between Midgley Moor and Warley Moor en route from Rain to Mist. The next leg towards Dew takes advantage of level walking and easy navigation by following the Leeds-Liverpool Canal, passing the extraordinary Bingley Five-rise Locks. Streams, reservoirs and waterfalls punctuate the journey, reminding the walker of how water shapes and animates the whole South Pennines.

Once the optimum route had been selected, walked and photographed, a measurement was taken to reveal a total length of 47 miles, rather a long way for a single trip but capable of being tackled one section at a time. In keeping with the environmental credentials of the project, public transport accessibility had informed route selection, so three manageable day-length walks take the walker from Marsden Railway Station to Ilkley Station, via Hebden Bridge and Bingley Stations.

Although each leg can be tackled on separate occasions, all sections involve at least some high-level walking on difficult terrain with moderate navigational skills required. In order to keep the key parts of the project, the carved stones themselves, within the capabilities of as broad an audience as possible a series of short walks was also devised. These adopt slightly different starting points where a car can be parked and groups such as families with children or elderly relatives can take their time, on relatively good ground and with simple directions, to reach an individual Stanza Stone in no more than half an hour.

Along the trail many resting opportunities present themselves, ranging from cosy pubs and cafés to exposed boulders in lofty vantage points, but the project has also introduced two distinctive, purpose-built seats. Close to Snow and with an expansive view over the upper Colne Valley, the Marsden seat announces in beautifully carved numerals a distance of 45¼ miles to Ilkley, a number replicated as the distance to Marsden on the seat's counterpart on the banks of Backstone Beck just outside Ilkley: it is evident that there is nothing to be saved by walking backwards from Ilkley to Marsden, so rest and be thankful!

Tom Lonsdale, Marsden, 2013

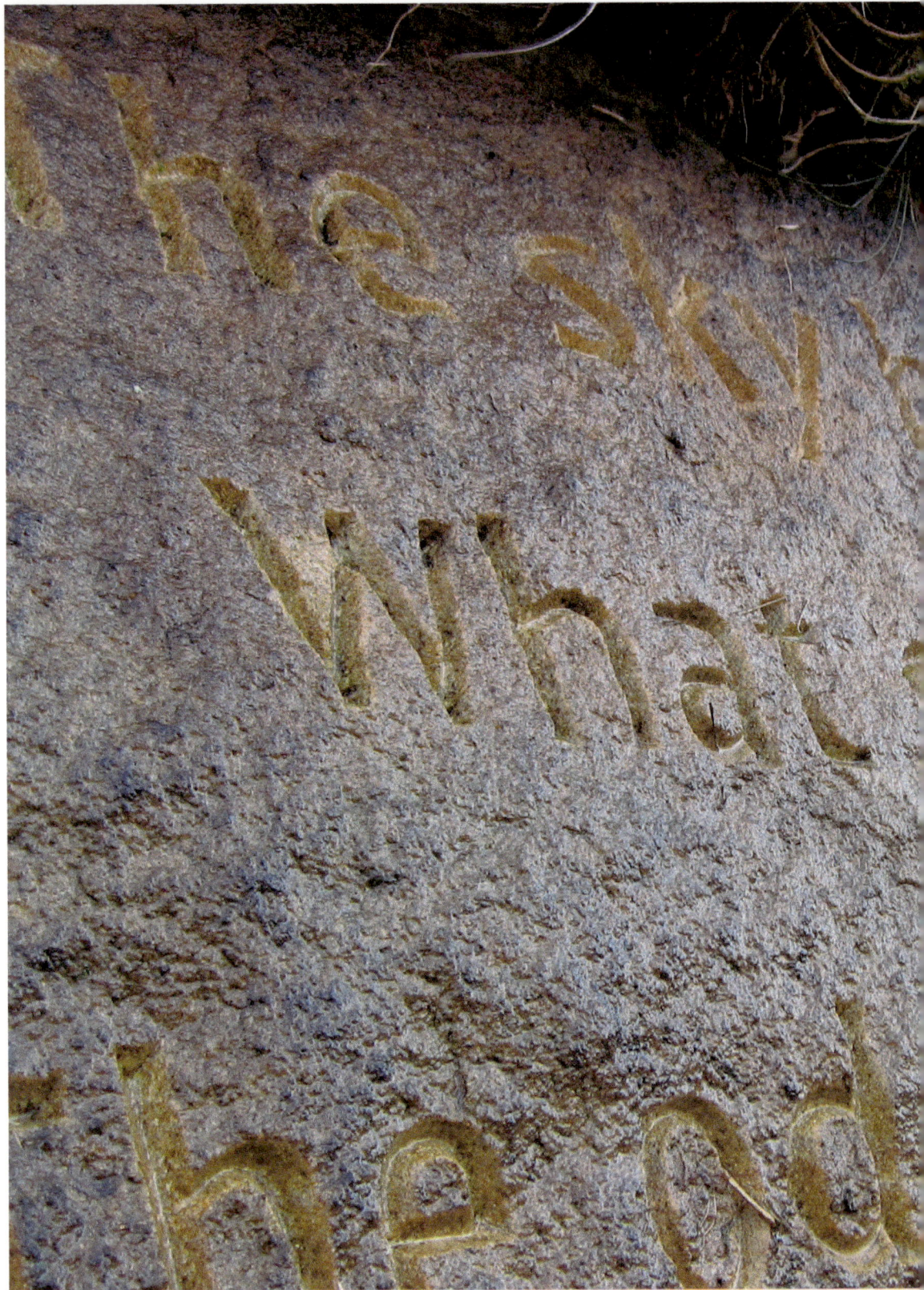

The sky

What

The

snow

...ered it's blank...

...all that colourless water can drink... Soon, like water...

...length of winter. We should...

...ral thousand slides and rides. Snow... now is how the snow...

Then it warms and weeps.

SNOW

The sky has delivered
its blank missive.
The moor in coma.
Snow, like water asleep,
a coded muteness
to baffle all noise,
to stall movement,
still time.
What can it mean
that colourless water
can dream
such depth of white?
We should make the most
of the light.

Stars snag
on its crystal points.
The odd, unnatural pheasant
struts and slides.
Snow, snow, snow
is how the snow speaks,
is how its clean page reads.
Then it wakes, and thaws,
and weeps.

SNOW

The sky has delivered its blank missive. The moor ... it mean that colourless water ... dream ... The odd ... where ... a coma. Snow, like water as ... such depth of white? We don't ... snow, snow is how the snow spells snow ... thaws and weeps.

THE QUARRY on Pule Hill is a remarkable time capsule, possessing a potent sense of arrested activity and a ghostly hint that quarrymen may reappear at any moment. So unusual is the state of interrupted working that a professional archæologist was commissioned by the National Trust to report on the site's sensitivity before consent was granted for the carving of the Snow Stone. 'Exclusion zones' were declared for the worked faces and abandoned structures, such as the engine housing used to winch stone down the associated incline.

The quarry faces are well used by rock-climbers and we were keen not to interrupt their routes or offend their values. The site seemed otherwise neglected, though footfall has increased since its inclusion in the Stanza Stones Trail, whilst the poem itself draws visitors into one of the more intimate enclosures: the carving adorns two huge slabs, stacked to support waste material, clearly intended to shelter quarrymen as they worked. So the poem can be whispered aloud in calm air even on the windiest of days.

TL

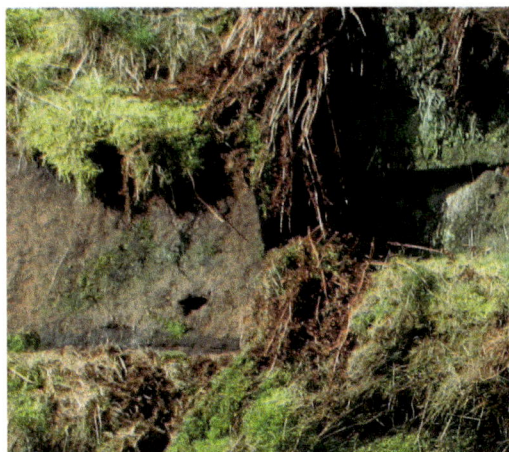

25 May *On Pule Hill with Simon and Tom for the laying-out of the first poem: a significant moment. We were all drawn to this stone – which turns out to be two stones separated by a sort of niche – a secret shrine behind a fern shroud. Arranging the words across this cleft connects the two slabs, and seems to add something to the poem's new physical form. Indeed Simon took advantage of this rocky lacuna and removed the word 'up' that until now he had felt was necessary after 'dream'. There are practical considerations, and to make it easier to read across, we space the lines widely and arrange them so that the gap falls mid-sentence.*

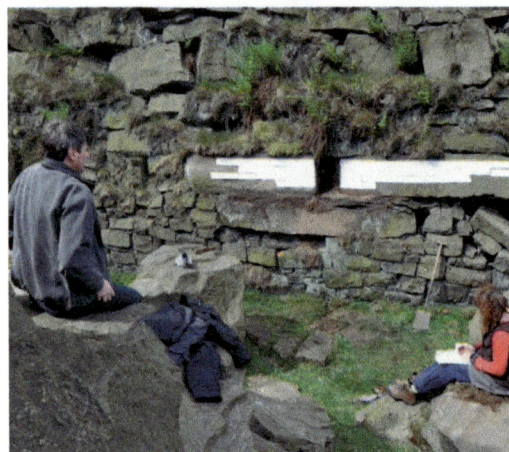

10 June *Warming up in the Carriage House bar after a 12-hour day at the rock face on Pule Hill. Tracing the poem onto the stone, the carbon paper barely showed up. I found a scrap of yellow dress-makers' 'carbon' paper, (added to the tool bag as an after-thought) which leaves just enough of a mark for me to go over the traced letters with colour pencil. Drawing on this rough stone, the pencils – 9H for tracing and watercolour for high-lighting – require a thumb-numbing grasp.*

11 June *Working last night in the fading light, I left it too late to high-light a good two hours' worth of tracing and I returned today to find that the rain had washed away all sign of it. However, the algæ which had added to my tracing problems was also drenched, and its sliminess made its removal easy. The newly cleaned stone is more receptive to the carbon, making the retracing a quicker job today.*

11 June *Simon visited, with his daughter Emmeline – and brought hot chocolate – for a final checking-over of my drawing and some essential proof-reading. And then I started carving the first Stanza Stone. The creamy-white of the cut letters shines out of the sooty-umber stone. Turning away from 'snow, snow, snow' to gaze at the muted sepias and rusts of the surrounding crags, it's startling to imagine them when they were freshly-exposed by the quarrying: the top of Pule Hill must have gleamed like a beacon.*

13 June *The wall in which my stones are set is reassuringly protecting against the weather. And I've discovered I am not the only one to settle on this secluded corner for a creative project: a mistle-thrush has moved in too, and is nesting, unperturbed, in her own rocky niche, just a few feet away from my hammering.*

14 June *Among the features in the stone that influenced positioning of the lettering were the small hollows cut in by the 19th-century quarrymen to help with manœuvring. The poem layout couldn't avoid these holes altogether, however, and so part of the day was spent levelling them out a bit, in order to make carving in them possible.*

15 June *A sun-filled day saw much activity on Pule, with climbers and a flock of hang-gliders, one of whom*

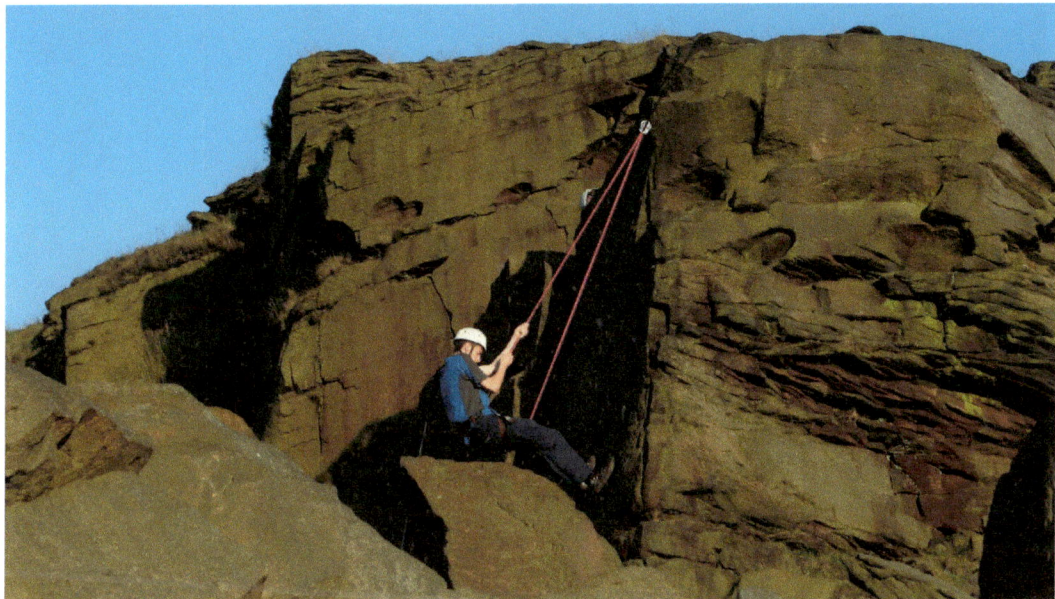

landed nearby, curious to get a closer look at what he had spotted from high above. I stayed till after 10pm, late enough that my stroll down the incline was shared with a prowling fox. Wayne arrives by train tomorrow to help me carve Snow.

30 June *Today I heard a Marsden lad, stood high up on the rocks behind me, reciting Snow to his girlfriend. To my comment that he must have good eyesight to see from that distance, he replied that he hadn't read from the stone but from a copy he'd made of the poem on a previous visit.*

The thrush chicks are growing well amidst their jumble of bracken and fleece in the wall: their mother's determination in her feeding task despite our noise and proximity is admirable.

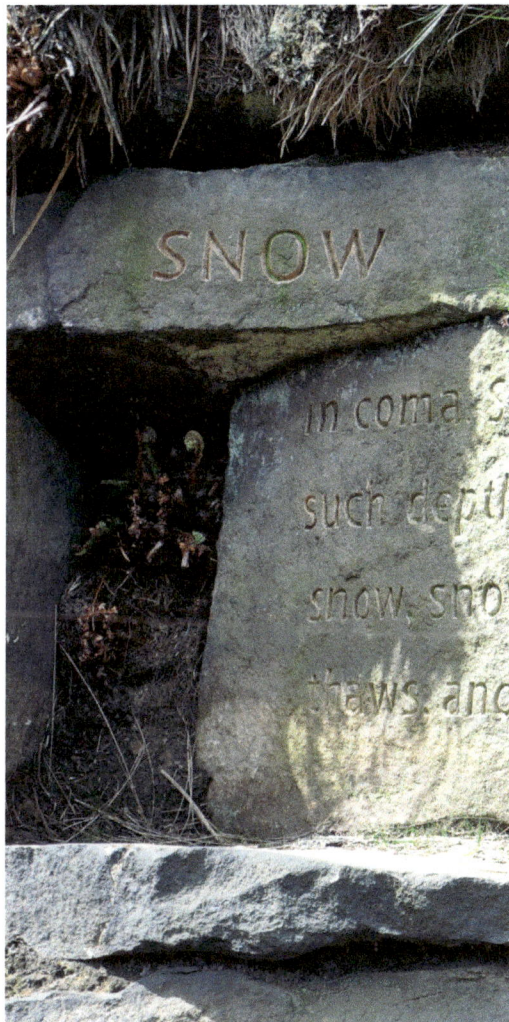

4 July *After fifty hours carving 330 letters, and another eighty hours spent in preparation, meetings, drawing and travelling, the first Stanza Stone is finished. The contrast between the newly-cut letters and the weathered stone is at its highest, and although I find this crisp, striking effect has its own appeal, it will be good to see Simon's poem 'settling in' over the next few months, through weathering and other natural processes: growing into the landscape.*

salty

a soft

ne rai

ld sea

bead a

ndrop

rain

ea...

then laundered a...

...it strafes in sheets, it is no mo...

...upon the tongue, tasting cloud pe...

...go hee where the front of the min...

RAIN

Be glad
of these freshwater tears,
each pearled droplet
some salty old sea-bullet
air-lifted out of the waves,
then laundered and sieved,
recast as a soft bead
and returned.

And no matter how much
it strafes or sheets,
it is no mean feat
to catch one raindrop
clean in the mouth,
to take one drop
on the tongue, tasting
cloud-pollen,
grain of the heavens,
raw sky.

Let it teem, up here
where the front of the mind
distils
the brunt of the world.

Be gla
each pearled
air-lifted out of the waves, then laundered and sie
And no matter how much it strafes or sheets, it is no mean f
to take one drop on the tongue, tasting cloud polle
let it teem up here where the front of the mind

RAIN

se freshwater tears,
some salty old sea-bullet
ast as a soft bead and returned.
atch one raindrop clean in the mouth,
n of the heavens, raw sky.
he brunt of the world.

SA

MOST OF the Stanza Stones Trail courses its way through West Yorkshire, but for a while, trail-walkers are afforded views across the metropolis of Greater Manchester, with the towns of Oldham and Rochdale directly below. Just east of Littleborough there is a handy pub called the White House, from which even the least energetic walker can stroll easily northwards along the Pennine Way, passing exposed reservoirs in the company of curlews and sandpipers. In the distance, a curious outcrop of rock seems to beckon as an obvious destination for turning around or as a marker along the whole trail.

It always takes longer to get there than expected but the effort is rewarded by a quaint little bridge just before the landmark is reached and the sculpted striations of the rock formation itself. A large part of the outcrop has been quarried away, with smooth slabs extending down into a big hole in the ground, leaving the virgin rock thrusting skyward at the southern end. Climbing routes swarm over much of the quarry faces and incised lettering could perhaps change the official grading quoted in the guide books. When invited to comment on options for siting a poem, the British Mountaineering Council expressed a preference for the sloping slab at the southern end, already identified as an ideal location by the project team. So Rain can now be read at eye level while taking a breather or pausing to eat a packed lunch, or even used as a backrest.

TL

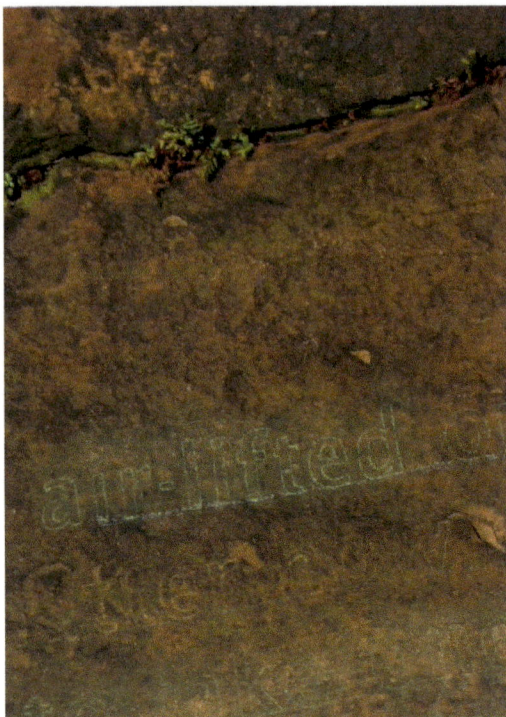

19 October *Simon and Emmeline arrived – with more hot chocolate – for viewing the layout of the paper ribbons of Rain. The great whale-like length of the rock means the letters can be much larger here than they are for Snow and Mist; their scale makes the poem legible from the footpath. We have our usual amicable exchange about straight and curving lines. Our views are in this case fairly academic since the rock, curving in all directions, distorts lines of any shape. I will spend the next few days tracing the drawings onto the rock.*

22 October *A wet start this morning though spirits undampened as I was*

greeted by a decorative display of sand trickling out of rain-rinsed 'Rain', streaking creamy patterns on the rock.

24 October *As we cut, this gritstone chips our chisels. Unlike the Mist and Snow stones, it glitters with quartz grains and we are learning to feel for those hidden beneath the surface, and soften the mallet blows in time to avoid damage. There are clues aplenty on our route here, as we crunch over pure white crystal beads sparkling in the black peat: these non-soluble minerals are all that's left after æons of rock erosion.*

25 October *Fine weather again and dramatic sunsets over Manchester. The late afternoon sun has turned the deep*

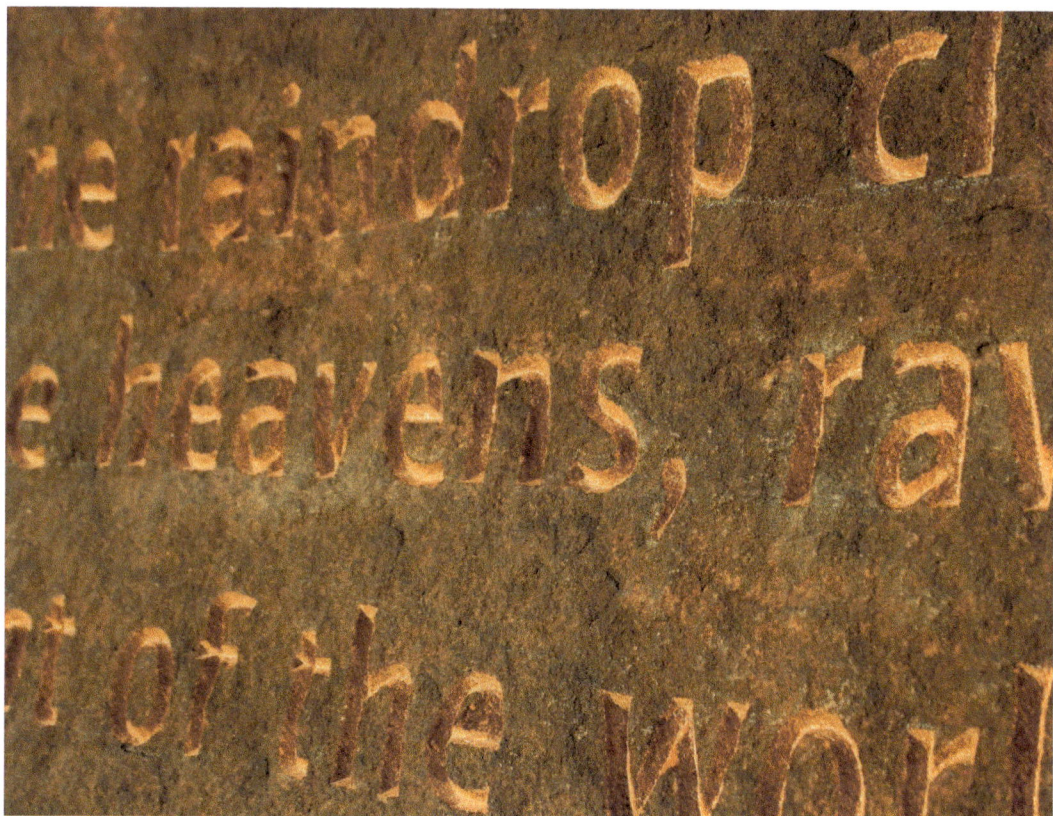

amber letters bright gold and they glow in the dusty umber rock.

26 October *Today a brief visit from a climber: wordlessly he joined me for a few moments' study of the rockface and then a swift ascent, fingers and toes nimbly finding their place among my carefully positioned letters before he disappeared above the gritty parapet.*

31 October *We receive regular visits from Jack Fearn, a local guardian of the Blackstone Edge moorland – and our most enthusiastic fan yet. An amateur rock carver himself, he claimed that he had learnt more watching us than in all the time he had spent carving, and therefore had better take us to the pub for supper. Amongst a host of colourful stories, Jack recalled how long ago he had taken his seven-year-old son up onto the moor with chisel and mallet to carve his initials in the gritstone – as a rite of passage.*

Who does it mean...
nearness, gathering
while your back was
net curtains around?
is water in its ghost
ing its milky breath,
f great cities under
hese moments, into
gritstone and peat
eing will seep into
l are lost adrift i

ere on th...
...ned, drawing...
...atureless silvers...
...ate, all inwardne...
...eiling the pulsing
...our feet, walling
...his anti-garden
...iven time the e...
...ts fibreless fur...
...hung water

mist

MIST

Who does it mourn?
What does it mean,
such nearness,
gathering here
on high ground
while your back was turned,
drawing its net curtains around?
Featureless silver screen, mist
is water
in its ghost state,
all inwardness,
holding its milky breath,
veiling the pulsing machines
of great cities
under your feet,
walling you
into these moments,
into this anti-garden
of gritstone and peat.

Given time
the edge of your being
will seep
into its fibreless fur;
you are lost, adrift
in hung water and blurred air,
but you are here.

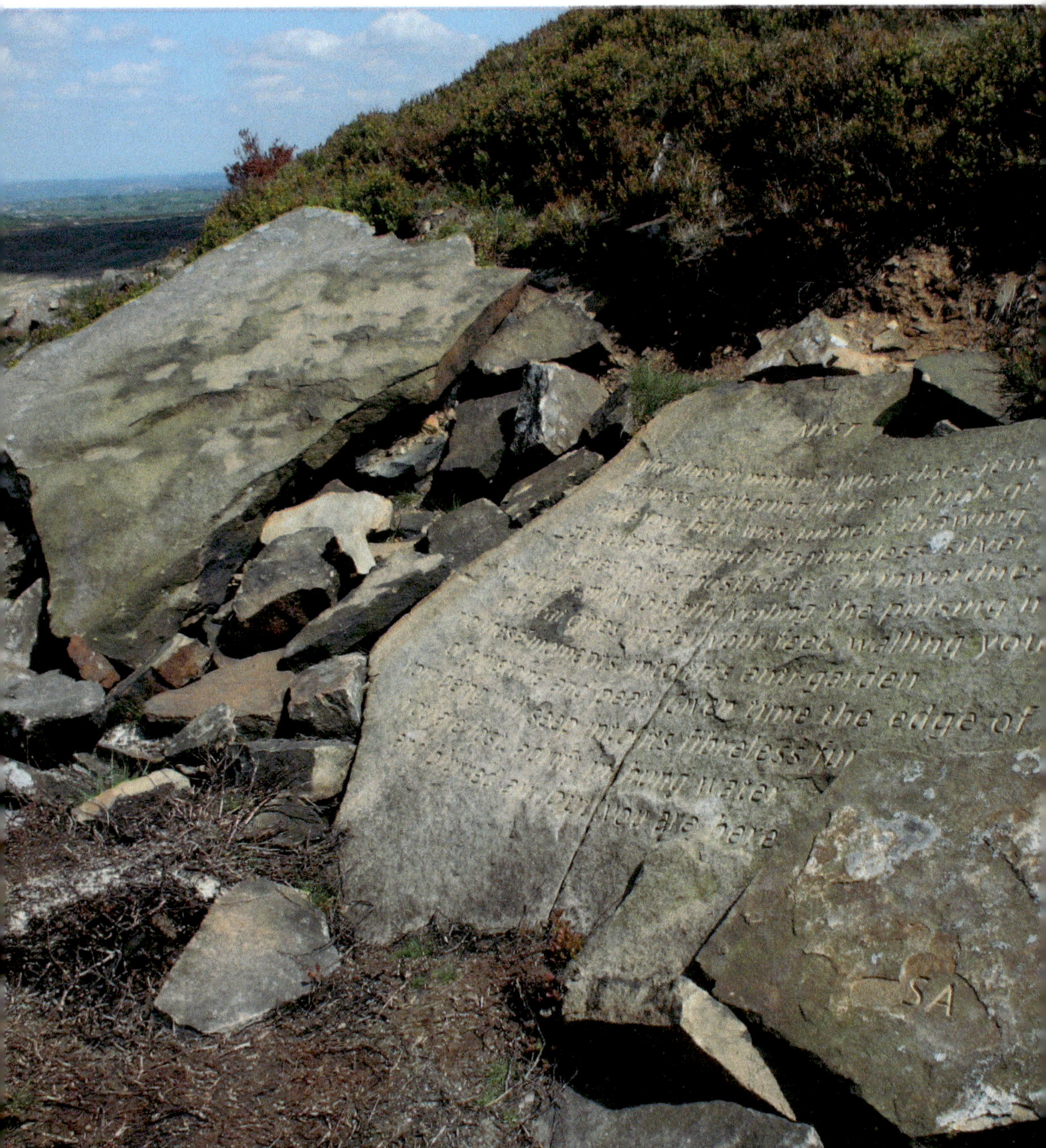

your feet, walling you
garden
time the edge of
are here
SA

FOLLOWING THE trail from Hebden Bridge
towards Bingley can be a moist experience because
Warley Moor rarely dries out, although a less
boggy walk along Cold Edge Lane suddenly opens
up distant views to the free-draining limestone of
Ingleborough and its neighbours. In the fore-
ground lies Oxenhope and above it a haunting
escarpment populated by cairns – freestanding
structures assembled by nameless builders from
the stone waste left over by delvers who quarried
Nab Hill for Yorkshire's distinctive roofing slates.

Most of this stone litter was unsuitable for
carving and a further three-dimensional form
might have set up tension with those existing
structures, so a larger prone form was chosen.
Several large slabs were located and the preferred
candidate selected for lifting so that Pip could
carve it without injuring her back. Yorkshire Water
issued a temporary licence, transferring to Ilkley
Literature Festival and its contractors 'possession'
of a small area of moor under strict working
methodology conditions approved by Natural
England. During lifting, this slab broke into two
along a pre-existent crack, resulting in Pip carving
the two parts independently and then reposition-
ing them on the ground to read as one.
TL

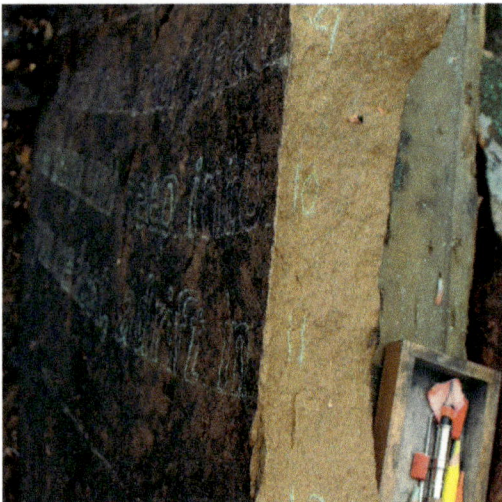

28 August *My plan to work on the Stanza Stones in sequence with the trail is adjusting to accommodate nesting-season restrictions, and so my next carving appointment will be at the Mist Stone on Nab Hill.*

1 September *A meeting with Tom and a crack team of piano-movers who will shift the Mist Stone into a position to make carving possible. Thoughts of the hairline fissure travelling down the middle of the stone have been making me uneasy about carving on this enormous slab. So it was a relief – to me at least – when, at the first attempt to lift the stone, it obligingly broke in two. Crunch. I had a job trying to reassure the mortified team that I was truly thrilled, because, far from creating a problem they had in fact solved one for me. The two pieces are now propped up high on the hillside, ready for drawing.*

2 September *A bright orange ring of security netting around the stone is the only sign visible from the road of my activity on Nab Hill this autumn.*

6 September *The stone surface is proving even less receptive to my carbon paper than the Snow Stone, and in my collection of emergency oil-pastels it is the orange that stands out best. I spent the afternoon scribbling it on the back of my drawings. Even so, tracing onto the stone left only the faintest marks, requiring a further process of highlighting*

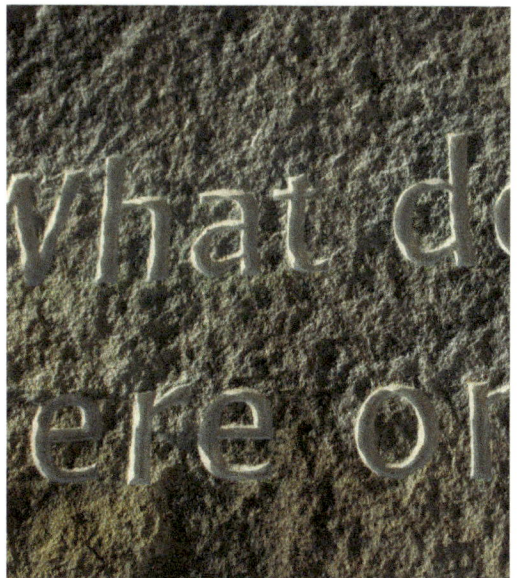

with waterproof pencil. My main concern however has been to ensure the gently curved lines will match up when the stones are reunited. The odd angles at which the two halves have been positioned means that drawing consistently curved guidelines involves a certain amount of guesswork, despite endless remeasuring and checking.

7 September *Simon and Tom visited. We are all delighted at the way the stone split so conveniently. At home in the dry, on a paper copy of the two stones,*

sketching out the lines of Mist across the cleft, I am reminded of Snow – the shape of the cloven stones in this case, however, connecting more with that of an open book.

9 September *The colour of the cut stone is a paler cream than that of Snow; the stone seems grittier, coarser in texture, and perhaps a bit softer.*

22 September *Fine autumn weather, and carving is well underway on the second Stanza Stone now Wayne has joined me. The letters are by now familiar: their carved forms are measuring out a steady, regular rhythm in counterpoint with the characterful, dappled Nab Hill rock. The position of the stones makes for some awkward carving positions, so until the removals team can return to adjust them, we have a system of swapping stones – and muscle-aches – every few hours.*

23 September *The views from the stones are expansive and exhilarating.*

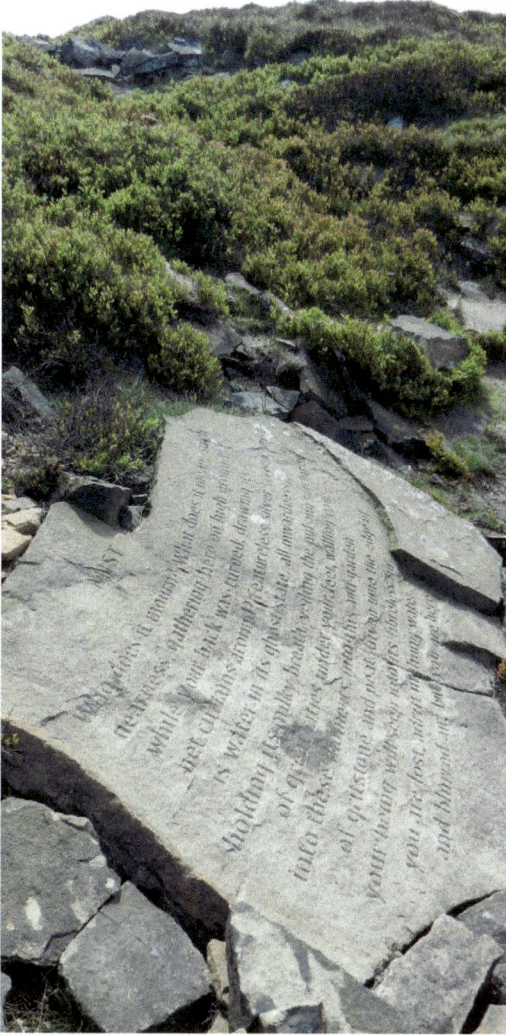

Northwards, my gaze drifts beyond Oxenhope towards Haworth: so easy to imagine the Brontë sisters, perhaps between chapters, or in search of inspiration, once striding this way.

28 September *Warm and bright again today, and we worked until sundown before heading for a rather luxurious B&B nearby (since we haven't quite got the camping temperatures we had for Snow).*

3 October *Replacing the stones was a straightforward job for the team, who carefully lowered the thin slabs, gravity's force only pulling them a matter of inches further down the steep terrain from their original position. Still uncertain about the two sets of poetry lines meeting in the middle, it was a tense moment for me. The extensive measuring has paid off, though, and only a couple of letters needed chiselling out and recarving – not an impossible task in such a rough material.*

The tense st
of summe
the touchy fu
of parche
ers of bulrush a

DEW

d-off
s end,
-wire
grass,
d reed,

dew

DEW

The tense stand-off
of summer's end,
the touchy fuse-wire
of parched grass,
tapers of bulrush and reed,
any tree
a primed mortar of tinder,
one spark enough to trigger
a march on the moor
by ranks of flame.

Dew enters the field
under cover of night,
tending the weary and sapped,

lifting its thimble of drink
to the lips of a leaf,
to the stoat's tongue,
trimming a length
of barbed-wire fence
with liquid gems, here
where bog-cotton
flags its surrender
or carries its torch
for the rain.

Then dawn, when sunrise
plants its fire-star
in each drop, ignites
each trembling eye.

SA 2012

DEW

The tense stand-off
of summer's end,
the touchy fuse-wire
of parched grass,
tapers of bulrush and reed,
any tree
a primed mortar
of tinder, one spark
enough to trigger
a march on the moor
by ranks of flame.

Dew enters the field
under cover of night,
tending the weary and sapped,
lifting its thimble of drink
to the lips of a leaf,
to the stoat's tongue,
trimming a length of barbed-wire fence
with liquid gems, here
where bog-cotton
flags its surrender
or carries its torch
for the rain.

Then dawn, when sunrise
plants its fire-star
in each drop, ignites
each trembling eye.

THE TWO Dew Stones stand on the divide between two very different worlds that were once one. The planting of conifer forest on part of Rough Holden, on Rivock Edge, has created over time a dark inner space, through which a bridleway leads travellers from cultivated fields to a stunning 'north window'. An enclosed tunnel with tree trunks to the side and a narrow slit of sky above suddenly turns sharply to the side and reveals a beautiful panorama over rough pasture to picturesque hills beyond; occasionally the rare hen harrier can be seen here quartering for prey. This threshold is emphatically marked by an ancient dry-stone wall, into which the Dew Stones have been deftly inserted with the poem halved between the two faces. A subtle gap separates the stones, not wide enough to permit sheep entering the forest or people to pass though but just wide enough for the eye to connect these two worlds and the consciousness to be drawn through.

TL

18 November *To Marshall's quarry at Brighouse again, with Tom, to view the stones I'd chosen for Dew on a previous visit. The quarry have sawn an enormous slab of Scoutmoor gritstone down the middle, so that the two halves open out like a book. The pieces now need shaping at the edges, and Tom, who knows about the weight capacity of the installation machinery, will offer guidance on maximum size, while I draw the shape I need for the poem.*

7 December, Dent *Today, the Dew Stones arrived at David's farm near my home in Dentdale, and friend Chris helped to manœuvre them into position, ready for carving. The sight of them sheltered and supported with straw bales in their temporary cow-*

shed 'studio' makes for a striking contrast with my moorland habitat. Their arrival marks a migration of the project from gritstone edge to limestone dale – and will mean an adjustment to my drawing process. Working in situ *I engage with the environment on many levels, and I naturally draw inspiration from my surroundings: this influences my designing and decision-making in subtle, unconscious ways. This means that working on stones away from their intended site, I am relying on my site-visit photos and sketches to create an inscription that will fit in with the landscape.*

22 December *Simon visited for a fruitful discussion about layouts – accompanied by Tom with camera.*

6 January 2012 *The uniformly flat carving surfaces of these 2-metre-high megalithic forms contrast sharply with the natural roughness of the Snow, Rain and Mist Stones, and echoes of the printed page are perhaps making me more mindful of Simon's inclination for straight lines. However, I think it would be good if the lettering helps to connect these machined 'off-comedens' with their intended home and so, while drawing guidelines for the poem, I shall keep in mind the distant rolling hills and the irregular courses of drystone walling of the Rivock Edge site.*

11 January *By now the Stanza Stones lettering style is very familiar to me, and during this off-site stage of carving, it is good to feel linked by it*

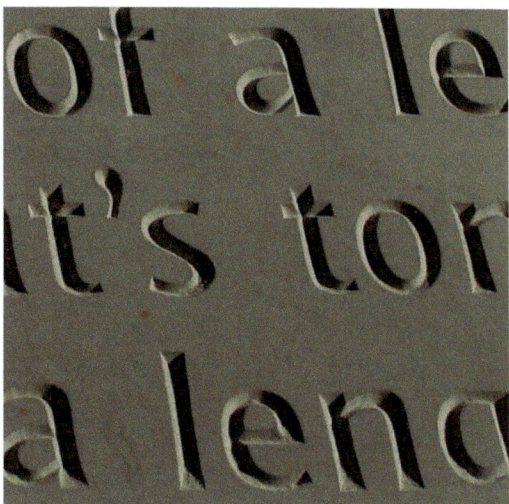

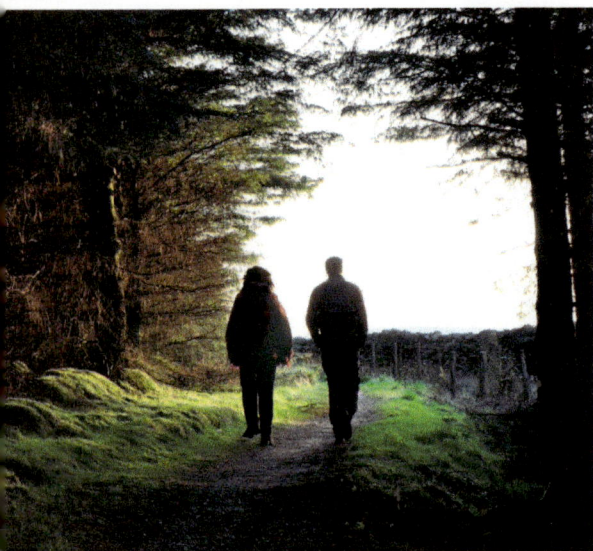

to the earlier part of the project up on the moors.

3 February *This stone, formed of the finest-filtered grains, is denser and harder than the moorland rocks. A repeat pattern in its silvery blue markings reminds me of traces left by the mild turbulence of waves on a sandy beach.*

4 March *The sun shone bright and warm, and the cows, having been*

DEW

The tense stand-off
of summer's end,
the touchy fuse-wire
of parched grass,
apers of bulrush and reed,
any tree
a primed mortar of tinder,
ne spark enough to trigger
a march on the moor
by ranks of flame.

Dew enters the field
under cover of night,
ing the weary and sapped,

lifting its thimble of drink
to the lips of a leaf,
to the stoat's tongue,
trimming a length
of barbed-wire fence
with liquid gems, here
where bog-cotton
flags its surrender
or carries its torch
for the rain.

Then dawn, when sunrise
plants its fire-star
in each drop, ignites
each trembling eye.

SA 2012

penned in for months at the back of the barn, got more and more restless. They eventually broke loose; Wayne and I dropped tools to escape the herd as they stampeded out of their winter confines and up into the sunny meadow, frisking and blinking in the unfamiliar light.

27 April *Today the Dew Stones were installed on Rivock Edge, in a grand performance involving the local* farmers and their enormous machinery, the whole Stanza Stones team as well as the student film crew – and the whole event skilfully co-ordinated by Tom. The stones are now standing in their gateway on the edge of the forest, permitting light through the narrow space between them. Signalling change, they will themselves become part of a changing landscape, as the forest is periodically cut down and replanted.

sho

puddle

PUDDLE

Rain-junk.
Sky-litter.
Some May mornings
Atlantic storm-horses
clatter this way,
shedding their iron shoes
in potholes and ruts,
shoes that melt
into steel-grey puddles
then settle and set
into cloudless mirrors
by noon.

The shy deer
of the daytime moon
comes to sip from the rim.
But the sun
likes the look of itself,
stares all afternoon,
its hard eye
lifting the sheen
from the glass,
turning the glaze
to rust.
Then we don't see things
for dust.

ROMBALDS MOOR is an enormous sponge that retains water long after its descent from the heavens, leading to many large puddles of the poem's title. Far from discouraging pedestrian movement, this bog witnesses regular human traffic and suffers seriously from ensuing erosion, so huge stone flags have been laid, end to end, to form a durable route that encourages walkers to keep off the embattled heather. These stones offered natural 'pages' for the poem but their precise position had to be carefully chosen to remain accessible while still capturing a sense of isolation and remoteness.

At virtually the highest point on the moor there is a large boulder, close to the new path and overlooking one of the largest puddles, from which a 360° view is available at all times but with a range determined by atmospheric conditions. On the day of installing the carved Puddle Stones, the mist was down and the heavy lifting machinery resembled alien creatures, capable of wreaking havoc but in the end positioning the stones with a surprising grace and a remarkable lightness of touch.

TL

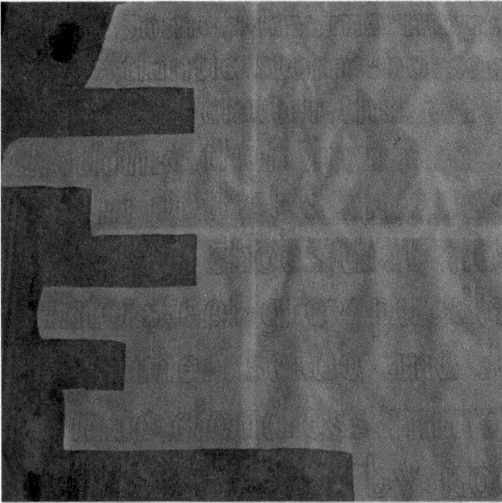

24 November *My third visit to one of Tony's reclamation sites, this time near Bolton, and after more clambering around scattered piles I think I have found our Puddle stones: two enormous flags. They have been lifted from the site of a 19th-century mill factory, and still show evidence of their former purpose in the rusting stumps of engine supports. The fine grain and softly pitted surface, levelled and honed by decades of clog-wearing machine workers, is just right for carving. Returning home, I mused over the story of the stones' journey: transported down from the moors in the industrial revolution to serve as flooring, in the 21st century they are about to be delivered back up there, to play their part in landscape poetry.*

14 December *Working on two pairs of stones in my temporary studio, I am aware of how much they differ from each other – in size, surface and in their intended positioning in the*

into steel-grey puddles
then settle and set
into cloudless mirrors
by noon

landscape. They have in common the layout of the poem with interrupted lines, as on a double-page spread, rather than continuing across the gap like Mist and Snow.

4 January 2012 *Close up to the Puddle Stones as I draw, I notice the marks on the surface have a curious rhythm, and I am struck by the way the words I'm drawing encourage a particular way of seeing the stone. I chose the stones for the poem, and yet the stones, with their rusty remnants and hoof-imprinted surfaces seem to be adopting the poem.*

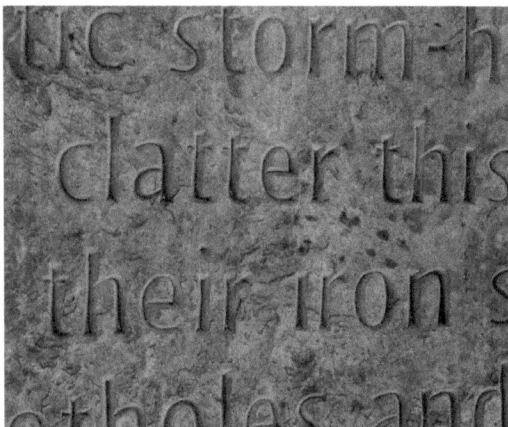

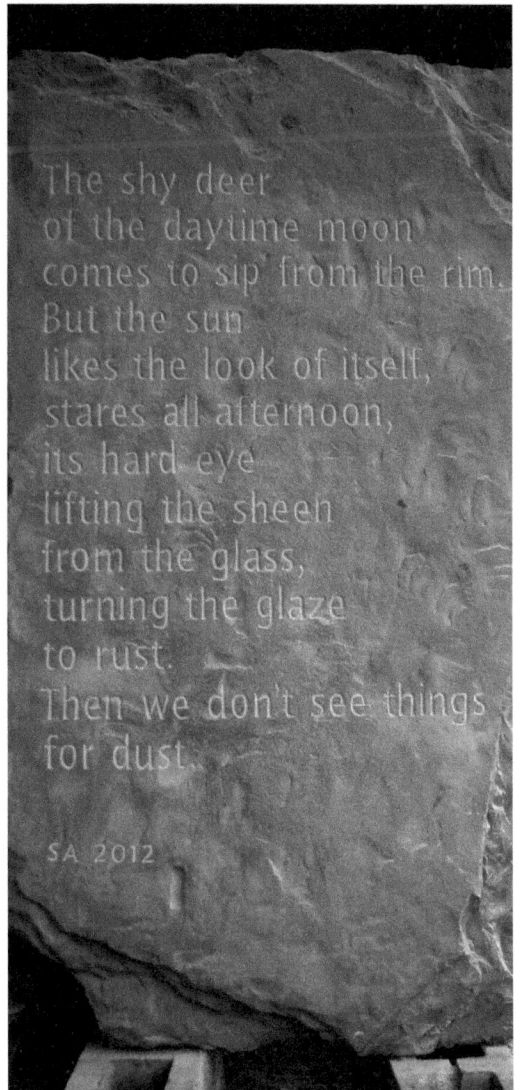

The shy deer
of the daytime moon
comes to sip from the rim.
But the sun
likes the look of itself,
stares all afternoon,
its hard eye
lifting the sheen
from the glass,
turning the glaze
to rust.
Then we don't see things
for dust.

SA 2012

14 March *The order of installing the two pairs of stones has been switched, so the Puddle Stones are leap-frogging their way onto the Pennine watershed, as we await a suitable date for the Dew Stones' installation. A misty atmospheric day as the teams gathered for setting the Puddle Stones up on Rombalds Moor.*

it back

more

from a

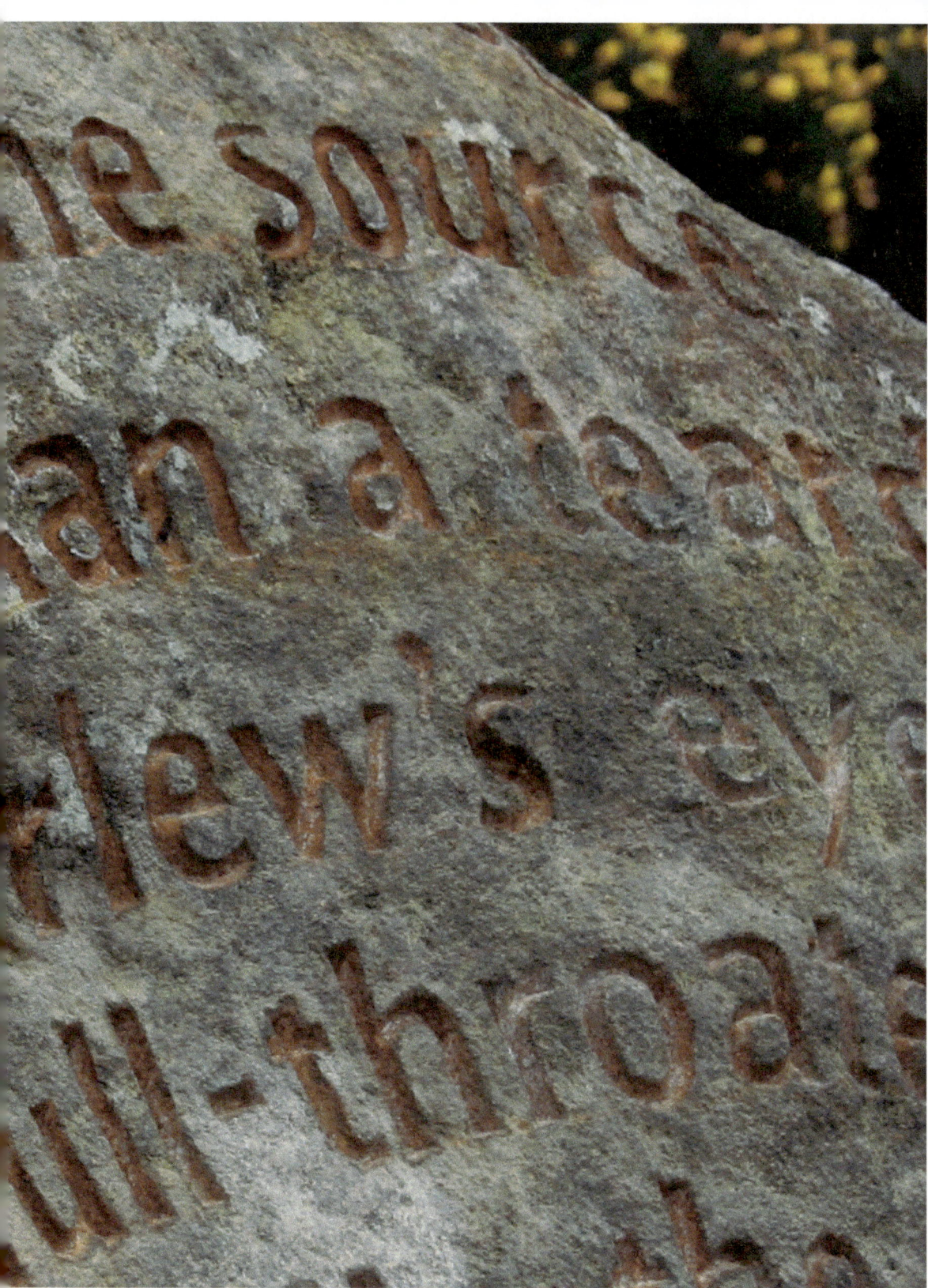

beck

Trace it back: the source
might be nothing more than a curlew's eye
squeezed from a ...
then follow it down to the full-throated roar
at its mouth – a dipper strolls the ve...
dressed for dinner in a white bib

The unbroken thread of the beck
with its nose for the sea
all flux and flex, soft-soaping a pebble
for thousands of years, or here
after hard rain, sawing the hillside in two
with its chain. Or here. Where water unhooks
and hangs at the waterfall's face as white...
...for that one stretched white instant
becomes ice

BECK

It is all one chase.
Trace it back: the source
might be nothing more
than a teardrop
squeezed from a curlew's eye,
then follow it down
to the full-throated roar
at its mouth:
a dipper
strolls the river
dressed for dinner
in a white bib.

The unbroken thread
of the beck
with its nose for the sea,
all flux and flex,
soft-soaping a pebble
for thousands of years,
or here
after hard rain
sawing the hillside in half
with its chain.
Or here,
where water unbinds
and hangs
at the waterfall's face,
and just for that one
stretched white moment
becomes lace.

IN THE Goitstock Wood section of the Trail, near Cullingworth, a splendid torrent cascades over a waterfall several metres high. Just above Ilkley, Backstone Beck tackles less onerous barriers to its downward progress by splashing playfully over and around an assortment of oddly shaped boulders. One of these resembles a large bar of soap and is wedged in the stream-bed at an angle perfectly suited to the display of text, claiming for itself the prize of Simon's words and the caress of Pip's chisel. Once our Beck Stone had been identified and all necessary permissions sought and obtained, Pip's happy lot was to immerse herself in the eponymous waters for several days to complete the watershed story.

TL

I was looking forward to carving Beck – the hot April days just like last year, cooling my feet off in the beck's refreshing trickle while chiselling in the welcome shadow of my sunhat. So mentally and sartorially at least I was not well prepared for the watery onslaught that was to mark the wettest carving experience not just of the project but of my career. It wasn't the rain directly (which was easily diverted with a gazebo) but its accumulation in Backstone Beck and subsequent cascade in which I had to submerge myself in order to work that provided my greatest challenge.

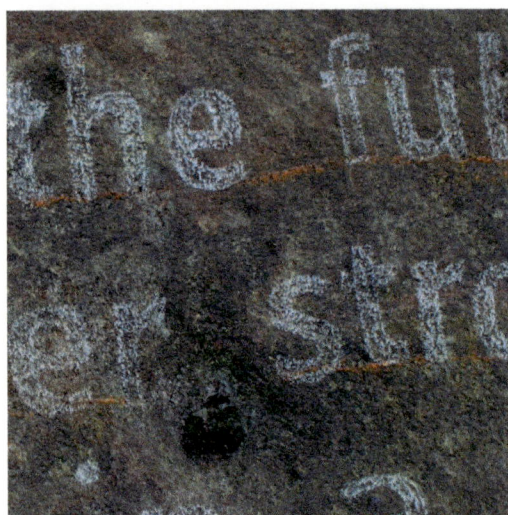

16 April *Six hours standing in the Beck Stone's waterfall, drawing the longest poem of the project: even though it didn't rain, I am soaked. New waterproofs tomorrow. A lively evening drying out, with Rachel and Glenis at the Cow & Calf, to mark the start of the final Stanza Stone carving.*

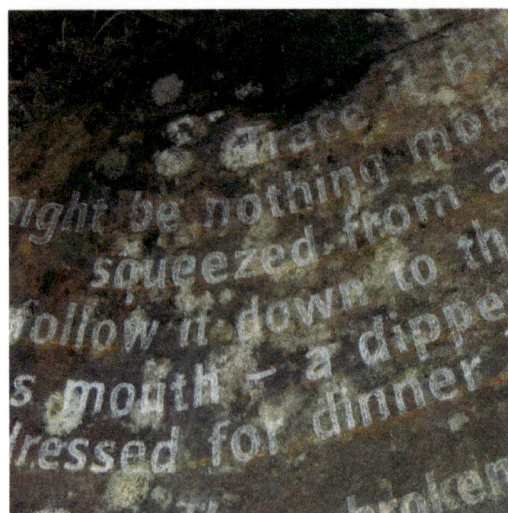

17 April *I'm drawing directly onto the stone rather than tracing from letters drawn on paper, and this direct contact means I am freer to follow the intricate changes in the rock's surface. However, it also means washing off and redrawing the lettering if Simon needs to edit. At this stage, having drawn over 2,000 of these letters, it won't be a lengthy task. The drawing is finished in its first state, though I am concerned about some crumbly areas on the rock, which I can't*

avoid. This is probably the softest of all the Stanza Stones (the next softest, if I had to order them, would be Mist, followed by Snow, then Rain, the fine-grained Dew and Puddle Stones being much the hardest to carve).

18 April Simon came to discuss the layout of Beck on the stone. This rock, more than the others, creates, as he says, a new template for the poem. Repositioning words to avoid the crumbly bits, there is a rewrite: this not only frees up some space, but also tightens the poem. The film crew arrived and recorded this collaborative moment as the rain began, before we all headed off to the Cow & Calf for lunch – and the chance of drying out. I was too complacent, lingering in the warm and dry, and by the time I got back to the stone the rain had dissolved much of my pencilling. I was grateful to Gail and Glenis helping me to assemble the gazebo, and the rest of the afternoon was spent painting over the lettering with acrylic.

23 April I arrived in dry weather, thrilled and alarmed in equal measure on seeing the wildness of the beck. Amazingly the gazebo is still in place – and the lettering has not been washed away as much as I feared. A call from Simon this morning about another alteration. He thought it would make things easier for me if 'over' were replaced with 'at' ('...water unbinds and hangs at the waterfall's face...'). I was pleased about a shorter word which would certainly help with the space issue; and far

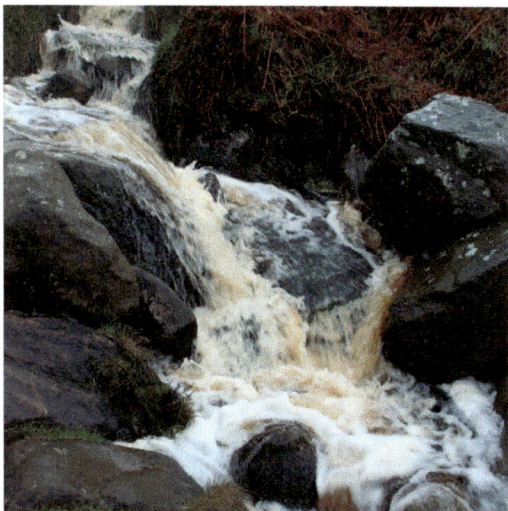

it is all
...ace it back
...ght be nothing more tha
squeezed from a curl
...hen follow it down to the futl
at its mouth — a dipper str
dressed for dinner In a

The unbroken thre
with its r
all flux and flex, soft-soapin
for thousands of years, or
after hard rain, sawing the hills
with its chain. Or here, where wate
and hangs at the waterfall's fac
or that one stretched white mo
becomes lace

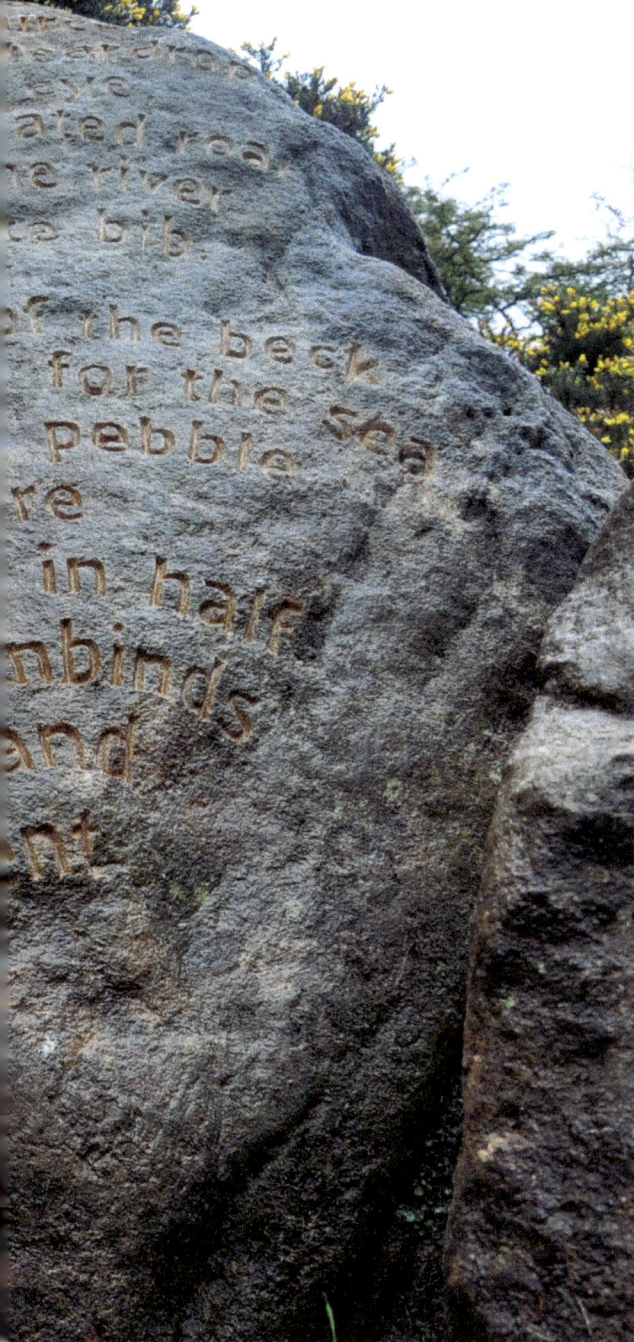

from compromising the poem, it is, as Simon explained, 'more active; visually and aurally lighter; gives it more tension.' Repositioning a couple of words I discovered how permanent the acrylic is, and am hoping a wire-brush will remove it.

24 April *Somehow a slow day. Weather better, and waterfall receding. Laura brought Rachel's husband David's drysuit this morning, which I just about squeezed into. This abysmal weather is making me feel grateful for rather a lot: the kindness and thoughtfulness of people – Rachel encouraging locals to visit, Glenis's Parkin, flasks as well as drysuit arriving, and, not least, the prospect of warm, dry and convivial evenings to look forward to, staying with Ellen, one of the Ilkley Literature Festival trustees.*

25 April *I am leaving the lowest two lines till last, in the hope that the waterfall level will drop enough for me to carve near the base of the stone without getting soaked. This exuberant beck, creeping higher by the day, is constantly washing away its own description. Meanwhile I have reached the soft end of the stone, where big grains fall away like biscuit-crumbs at the chisel's touch.*

For some reason I am not surprised to hear a second visitor this week tell me that her husband's ashes are scattered up here. It feels like the unending life-force of the beck has much to do with the powerful sense of place that draws people here.

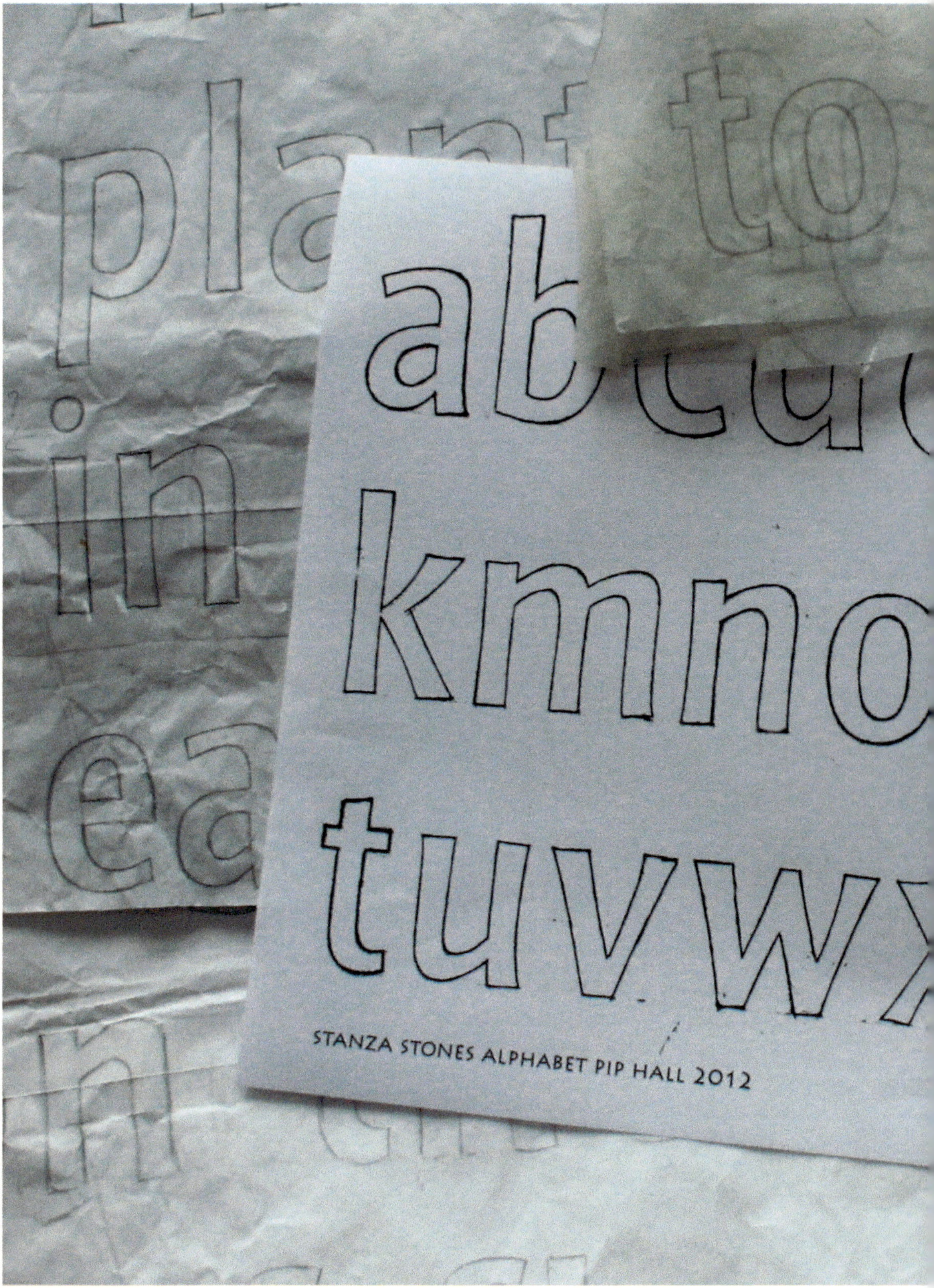

abcd
kmno
tuvwx

STANZA STONES ALPHABET PIP HALL 2012

plan to
in
ea

lettering and rock: pip hall

lettering

IN CHOOSING the Southern Pennine rock we were also choosing, or at least setting limits on, letterform and layout. The gritstone's demand for a plain, sans serif form was echoed by Simon's requirement for a clear, unobtrusive visual rendering of his poems.

Knowing from carving experience that 'gritstone' is something of a convenient umbrella term, I'd been uncertain about just what the rocky outcrops of the moors would hold in store for a lettercarver. Cutting a few trial letters in a rough fragment from the northern tip of the proposed poetry trail confirmed that for lettering to be clearly visible in the coarse texture, it would need to be bold and simple in design. It also gave me some idea of likely carving speed – useful information for a project this size.

Subsequent stimulating discussions with Simon gave me further guidelines for my drawing. Our conversation, rambling around the nature and definition of lettering, fonts and typefaces, prompted in me a more analytical exploration of the forms I draw and their sources. My brief was to design lettering which, in its plainness and neutrality would avoid imposing its own character on the meaning of the poem. Since my instinct in drawing lettering is concerned with exploring form and expressing ideas, I found it helpful to think of the lettering more as a vessel for the poetry rather than being too present in itself. My first designs for the Stanza Stones letters were plain, bold sans serifs, well-spaced with minimal variation of stroke width, aiming at restraint and stillness. Nonetheless they got the thumbs-down from Simon, who seemed concerned that they might suggest something was lacking in the poetry. 'Too curly' was his verdict.

Setting about straightening the already subtle curves in my letterforms, I tried to imagine the strong contrast of straight lines cut into the coarse rock. Replacing curves with horizontal lines, such as in the e; keeping junctions within letters open; and levelling out arms of letters such as c, e, t and r had a quietening effect; there was less of the calligrapher's broad edge and more of the typefounder's art in the paring down of forms – in keeping with the eloquent sparseness of Simon's poetry.

Thus I eventually arrived at a lettering style we both felt happy with. We agreed right at the start that it should be common to all poems, that it would play an important role in connecting the Stanza Stones across the Pennines.

rock

Having learnt from the chisel something of the great range of gritstone to be found in one small area on the Southern Pennine watershed, it is instructive to find that the National Geological Survey identifies over thirty separately named types in its Millstone

Grit Group (lithodiversity reigned in the Namurian stage of the carboniferous). Of the seven I've carved, one is instantly recognisable: Pule Hill Grit is among the dozen sandstones of the Marsdenian substage. Over 300 million years old, these equatorial delta-formed sandstones might be defined by their mineral composition and present locality. To us lettercarvers, they are distinguished by subtle differences in texture and density, and occasional glittering crystal grains which affect our work, and we might describe them as biscuity, sticky, crumbly, as well as hard or soft. Especially surprising and delightful to me is the colour of the cut rock, and its contrast with the weathered surface, which varies from pale honey in peaty chocolate and silver in mottled blue-grey, to a glowing rufous gold in purple umber.

collaborating

Although we had arrived at a layout in principle by emailing text superimposed on photos of the stone, it wasn't until we were at the site that we could make detailed decisions about letter size, line-space and line-breaks. I would turn up with Simon's poem drawn full-size on long ribbons of paper and we would chop them up and fit them on the stone with gaffer tape. This system made it easy to rearrange line-breaks and line-spacing – as well as prompting occasional editing from Simon. It also somehow allowed my tendency for fluid lines and Simon's preference for straight ones (quite understandable for a poet more familiar with the conventions of the printed page) to find a resolution.

stone-pairing

Nothing in the poems pointed to them being carved on pairs of stones, and yet for very different reasons this is just how our choice of stones came about in most cases: the stone we all fell for, for Snow, turned out to be two blocks; the site for Dew gave Simon the idea for a pair of gate posts; later our Mist stone split in two,

and on Ilkley Moor, the size of the causey paving slabs meant that
we would need two for Puddle to fit. It felt serendipitous that this
companionable theme offered hints of the printed page. And is it a
complete coincidence that the Dew Stones are sited in view of the
ancient Doubler Stones on Rombalds Moor?

In their incipient form, Simon's poems appeared as vertical
columns of short lines on an A4 page, yet they were intended for
landscape-format stones: one of the most interesting aspects of
the project was being involved in the metamorphosis of the poems
from typescript to the realm of landscape, and witnessing how
the rocks we chose played their part in editing and designing
Simon's poetry.

The diverse aspects of this project made for a very enriching
experience of discovery and insight – from collaborating with
Simon, Tom and Rachel, exploring the moors and choosing the
stones, to working outdoors in a breathtaking part of the country,
and meeting so many interesting and enthusiastic people – and
with the assistance and company of my apprentice Wayne Hart.
The rock in which I had cut my trial letters was a fragment I'd
taken from Backstone Beck before my interview – with a murmured

promise to return it if I was given the job. At the end of the project I was reminded of this and so planned this postscript event for the day of the final Stanza Stones celebration, when the team would be converging at the Beck – and most probably for the last time (the date, happening to fall on Bloom's Day, was privately synchronous, since the fragmentary words I had chosen to cut were of a watery phrase from Joyce's *Ulysses* that I was delighting in at the time).

The returning of the stone that had helped to secure my place on the Stanza Stones team was accompanied by the 'hiding' of a stony memento. These stone slabs were split from a single block which I'd found in Backstone Beck during my semi-submerged carving. They form my personal thank-you to Simon, Tom and the Ilkley Literature Festival team, and celebrate a truly unforgettable project.

Pip Hall, March 2013

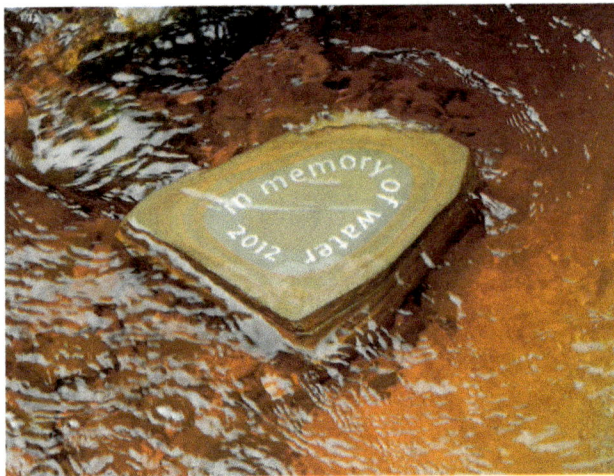

Stanza Stones
has been designed by Pip Hall
and printed by CPI Antony Rowe, Chippenham.
The typeface is ITC Baskerville and the text has been
printed on 130gsm Essential Velvet.

The first edition consists of 2500 hardback copies.

The signed limited edition,
bound and slipcased by The Fine Book Bindery,
is limited to fifty signed copies numbered 1 to 50
and twenty *hors commerce* copies numbered i to xx.